24:10

christopher idone
with helen m^ceachrane

Illustrations by Paula Munck

Cook
Capri

A PANACHE PRESS BOOK
CLARKSON POTTER / PUBLISHERS
NEW YORK

Published by Clarkson N. Potter, Inc.,
201 East 50th Street, New York, New York 10022.
Member of the Crown Publishing Group.

CLARKSON N. POTTER, POTTER and colophon
are trademarks of Clarkson N. Potter, Inc.
Manufactured in Japan
Design by Elizabeth Van Itallie

Library of Congress Cataloging-in-Publication Data
Idone, Christopher.
Cooking Caribe/Christopher Idone
with Helen McEachrane.—1st ed.
1. Cookery, Caribbean. I. McEachrane, Helen. II. Title.
TX716.A1I36 1992   91-30597
641.59729—dc20   CIP

ISBN 0-517-57664-3
10 9 8 7 6 5 4 3 2 1
First Edition

For their children—
the joys of Janet, Linda and Catherine—
and for every water baby who placed one
little foot into a tropical sea,
felt the sand beneath,
discovered a shell and then a world.

CONTENTS

Down the street from where I live,

there is a grocer who sells sugarcane, thick yams, plantains and West Indian pumpkins. There are blush-red mangos, pale green papayas split open to reveal jet-black seeds centered in a pool of golden flesh, and passion fruit with skin the color of eggplant, exuding a scent as heady as jasmine in the tropical night. There are green cherimoya, shaped like chiseled wooden pinecones, textured like custard, and tasting like sweet honey and cream with an added subtle flavor hinting of every tropical fruit I know. And in the shop freezer, big bags of peeled and pitted mangos, papaya, tamarind, soursop and guava sit next to the frozen peas, corn and okra.

My grocer is in the middle of Manhattan, far away from any enchanting island where most of this exotica can be bought at the local market, or even picked off a backyard tree. Caribbean fruits and vegetables have entered the global marketplace and are available in stores from Miami to Tokyo, from Los Angeles to Berlin. What's more, the Caribbeanization of American street food can be felt in most metropolitan areas across the country. Roti, the flat crêpelike Indian bread from Trinidad, is wrapped around curried meat or vegetable fillings and sold during lunchtime hot off vending trucks, from Wall Street to the downtown business district of Los Angeles. Pushcarts are filled with the aroma of spicy jerked pork and chicken, and hole-in-the-wall restaurants dish out empanadas and Cuban sandwiches piled hero-high with cheese and meats.

In metropolitan New York, the Caribbean population has exploded in the past two decades. The sounds of accented English, Creole, French and Spanish announce a world distinct from other ethnic enclaves. Bars, travel agencies, beauty salons, laundries and *bodegas* display in words, symbols and national colors each proprietor's island of origin.

Increasingly, restaurants with names like Sugar Reef, Bahama Mama, and Caribe advertise spicy jerk pork and chicken, Jamaican pastries, codfish cakes and peas and rice. These eating establishments evoke all the juice and jazz of the islands with touches that can include sand on the floor, coconut palms tacked to the ceiling and murals that describe a *faux* tropical paradise. The sounds of Trinidadian calypso, Puerto Rican salsa, Jamaican reggae, and souk, all the rage in both Martinique and Guadeloupe, accompany the food and spill out into the streets.

The genealogy of Caribbean cuisine starts with the peaceful Arawak Indians, who sailed northward from South America. They were the original island settlers, and they cultivated root crops and corn. Adept at catching and cooking fish and water fowl, they baked, stewed, smoked and roasted their meat, frequently seasoning it with *cassareep*, a condiment concocted from cassava juice, sugar and spices. These settlers were followed by fierce Carib hunters, who ate much the same as the Arawaks, but used no salt and seasoned their food with hot pepper sauces and lemon juice.

Culinary change came with Columbus's discovery of the West Indies. The Spaniards brought their staple, rice, and along with the Portuguese, were responsible for the introduction of codfish. Salted cod was stored in the ship's hold from Europe to the New World. It traveled well and fed the crew and colonists, hungry for familiar tastes. Even today, codfish is popular in dishes like *brule johl* (the cod salad from Trinidad), *féroce d'avocat* (the spicy spread from Martinique and Guadeloupe that includes mashed avocado and chili peppers) and the fritter that vendors call *bacalaitos* in Puerto Rico and *stamp and go* in Jamaica.

In the formative days of this cuisine, various dishes became signposts for their places of origin. *Empanadas,* flaky meat or chicken turnovers, traveled from Spain to the New World. *Asopao,* a stew of chicken or shellfish with rice, is served in Cuba, Puerto Rico and the Dominican Republic. *Bistec la Criolla,* a marinated steak popular in Cuba, is equally popular in Puerto Rico where the marinade—which they call *adobo*—includes Seville orange juice. Garlic and olive oil were kept for the meat stews, daubes, blaffs and *soupes de poisson* beloved by the French on the islands of Guadeloupe and Martinique. And their *boudin*—blood sausages spiced high with local ingredients and Scotch bonnet peppers—were à la Français counterpoint to the paler blood puddings preferred by the English in Trinidad and Barbados. The British, true to their homeland, served haunches of roasted meat, Yorkshire pudding and Christmas cake all year round. But it took African and Indian influences to give these island dishes zing and zest. The Dutch combined their dishes with local specialties, filling Edam cheeses with shrimp or beef, adding raisins, peppers, sweet pickles, pimientos and olives. Smoked fish like eel and herring appeared at table—so did *boterkoek,* a simple shortbread served with tea.

African slaves brought beans and *callaloo*, the leaves of the dasheen and malanga roots. The soup that bears its name is made in myriad variations from Jamaica to the French Antilles. Post-emancipation, laborers were imported from China and India to work in the sugarcane fields. The Chinese contributed a roster of staples, from spring rolls to chop suey. The Hindu influence is stronger in Trinidad, Martinique and Guadeloupe, where the introduction of *colombo* (or curry powder) added verve to the local culinary repertoire.

So, what is offered here is a panoply of signature dishes indigenous to these islands. Their authenticity derives from the legacy of my collaborator, Helen McEachrane, a native of Trinidad, whose childhood was marked by her mother's memorable cooking. Later in London and New York, Helen adapted these recipes for Anglo-American kitchens and palates, keeping alive in them the Caribbean flavor.

The impact of this wonderful patchwork cuisine on me had its roots in another time. I remember an early-morning walk I took in the seventies from Port-au-Prince to Petionville, just above the Haitian capital. I followed a muddy path to the local market where a bounty of live chickens, rabbits, quail and pigeons were displayed in stalls next to a little stand crammed with crocks of puddings and sausages and cascades of vegetables. There were herbs galore—chives and scallions, thyme, rosemary and parsley—a rainbow of hell-hot peppers and baskets filled with pineapples, mangos, coconuts, passion fruit, bananas, fresh cashew nuts and sacks of spices. All of this chockablock with panniers of lilies, roses, jasmine, tuberoses, oranges and limes. The profusion of smells and scents erupting in the air, the cacophony of noise and the brio of vendors and shoppers, the riot of colors popping out of shade and into dazzling sunlight—it was all stunning, like being hit by a tree in a hurricane.

Later, after my lunch of sun-dried turkey, deep-fried plantains, pork bits served with a fiery sauce called *ti-malice,* and red snapper seasoned with shallots, onions and hot peppers—the whole lot washed down with rum—I realized I was experiencing the culinary history of an island world crowded with so many cultures that it took my breath away. This book has been in my mind ever since.

CHRISTOPHER IDONE

Notes on Terms That May Be Unfamiliar

**Acrats, Accra,
Stamp and Go, Bacalaitos**
Spicy-hot fritters popular throughout the Caribbean. Methods, ingredients and names vary from island to island.

Allspice, Pimienta
Dark-brown berry, similar in size to juniper, that combines the flavors of cinnamon, clove and nutmeg.

Annatto, Anato, Achiote
Prickly pod with deep crimson-orange pulp surrounding a seed, used in making cooking oils. The dried seed adds bright coloring to dishes. Paprika serves as a substitute.

Arrowroot
Neutral-tasting starch extracted from the root of tropical tubers, used as a last-minute thickening agent for sauces.

Bay Rum
The bay rum tree is related to the evergreen that produces allspice. Used to flavor soups, stews and, particularly, blaff, the small dark bay rum berry is called "maleguetta pepper" in the French West Indies.

Beans, Peas
Interchangeable terms for red kidney beans, black beans, black-eyed peas, pigeon peas (*gandules*), and yellow and green lentils. Often combined with rice, used in soups and stews or pulped and made into fritters.

Bistec a la Criolla
Marinated steak—typically rump, round or sirloin of beef.

Blaff
A broth infused with whole Scotch bonnet peppers and bay rum leaves in which whole or filleted fish is poached.

Boudin, Black Pudding
Sausage that may include pigs' blood, thyme and Scotch bonnet peppers. Frequently served with souse, a pork dish that can include any part of the pig.

Buñuelos
Similar to crullers, they are made with flour, cassava meal or mashed sweet potato and have fruit fillings like guava and banana.

Carambola, Star Fruit
Tart or acidy-sweet star-shaped fruit used in desserts, as a garnish for drinks, tossed into salads or cooked together with seafood.

Calabaza, West Indian Pumpkin
Terms for a number of large squashes or pumpkins used in island stews and vegetable dishes. Hubbard and butternut squash are similar in flavor and make the best substitutes.

Callaloo, Callilu, Calaloo

Young green leaves of the edible tubers malanga and dasheen. *Callaloo* is the principal ingredient of the celebrated island soup of the same name. Spinach, kale, or a combination of two-thirds Swiss chard and one-third spinach are acceptable substitutes.

Cassareep

Made from the juice of grated cassava root and flavored with cinnamon, cloves and sugar—this is the essential ingredient in pepperpot, the ubiquitous Caribbean island stew.

Cassava, Yucca, Manioc

Root vegetable similar in length and shape to a turnip, with scaly yamlike skin. Universally made into flour for breads and cakes, and used as a base for tapioca and cassareep.

Cherimoya

Pale-green fruit with white sweet flesh that has the texture of flan. Used for mousse and fruit sauces, the fruit is best when fully ripe, well chilled and eaten with a spoon.

Chili Peppers

Members of the *Capsicum* genus ranging from medium to fiery hot. Scotch bonnet pepper, the most widely used, can be replaced with serrano, jalapeño or other hot peppers.

Chorizo

A Spanish sausage that combines pork, hot peppers and garlic, and is similar to longaniza.

Christophine, Chayote, Cho-cho, Mirliton

A small pear-shaped vegetable, light green or cream colored, and often covered with a prickly skin. Bland, similar in texture to squash and used primarily as a side dish or in gratins and soufflés. Like pawpaw (papaya), it is also a meat tenderizer.

Coco Quemado

A pudding similar to flan. Also a base for ice creams and a replacement for crème anglaise.

Conch, Lambi

Large Antillean mollusk with a spiral shell and brilliant pink interior. A popular ingredient in island fish dishes, the flesh is pounded to tenderize it before cooking.

Canned Sweetened Condensed Milk

Often caramelized in boiling water and served like a flan. Also used to sweeten coffee and to replace cream in many desserts.

Coo-coo

The Caribbean equivalent of polenta or grits. Once based on cassava or manioc meal, it is now made almost exclusively with cornmeal. Versatile coo-coo can be baked, fried or rolled into little balls and poached in soups or stews.

Coriander, Cilantro, Chinese Parsley

Intense, pungent herb that looks like parsley. The seeds are used in curries.

Creole, Criolla

Creole refers to the cooking of the French-speaking West Indies, as well as to southern Louisiana and the Gulf states. *Criolla* refers to the cuisine of Spanish-speaking islands. Both terms encompass a melding of ingredients and cooking methods from France, Spain, Africa, the Caribbean and America.

Dhal

Hindu name for legumes; in the Caribbean, it refers only to split peas or lentils.

Darne

The Caribbean name for kingfish.

Dasheen, Taro

Edible root of the taro plant, with dark brown skin, white or gray flesh, and a slightly nutty flavor. Dasheen is peeled and boiled in salted water, and then creamed, roasted or fried.

Escabeche

The Spanish word for "pickled." It usually refers to fresh fish (and sometimes poultry) that is fried, then pickled in vinegar, spices, hot peppers and oil.

Guava, Guayaba

Tropical fruit that has over a hundred species. It is pear-shaped, round and oval; yellow to green skinned, with creamy yellow, pink or red granular flesh; and has rows of small hard seeds. The smell and taste are intense and perfumy. Guava is used green or ripe in punches, syrups, jams, chutneys, ice creams and an all-island paste known as guava cheese.

Hearts of Palm

Ivory-colored core of some varieties of palm trees.

Hibiscus, Flor de Jamaica, Sorrel

A tropical flower—not to be confused with the garden-variety hibiscus—grown for its crimson sepal, which is used to flavor drinks, jams and sauces. It is available dried and fresh during the Christmas season.

Malanga, Yautia

A relative of dasheen or taro, this tuber is prevalent throughout the Caribbean.

Mango

Green at first, turning yellow, pink or crimson-green as it ripens. Strong exotic scent and sweet taste when ripe. Eaten plain or used in jams, ice cream, drinks, relishes, mousses, flans and compotes. Stewed and grilled green to accompany meat or fowl dishes and for chutneys.

Morue

The French name for codfish.

Okra, Okroes, Bhindi, Lady's Fingers, Gumbo
This finger-shaped vegetable, green-ridged and three to five inches in length, is fried as a side dish, used as a thickening agent in *callaloo* or mixed with cornmeal to make coo-coo.

Papaya, Pawpaw
All-island sweet fruit with rosy or golden flesh. Green, it can be stuffed and baked or used in jams, marinades, sauces, juices and desserts. It is also touted as a meat tenderizer and a digestive.

Passion Fruit, Maracudja, Granadilla
Oval-shaped fruit that has a tough shell and a color range from yellow-purple to eggplant to deep chocolate. The golden-yellow pulp is sweet and tropically exotic, and must be strained to remove the seeds. Used primarily in juices, desserts, drinks and sauces.

Picadillo
Spicy Cuban hash, made of ground beef and cooked with olives and raisins.

Pickapeppa Sauce
A commercial hot pepper condiment used to spice up food.

Plantain
Technically a banana-family fruit, but generally regarded as a vegetable. Inedible raw, cooked plantains are served as appetizers or starchy side dishes. The unripe (green), ripe (yellow) and very ripe (dark) plantains are used in Caribbean cooking. They become slightly sweet as they ripen.

Seville Orange
A bitter-sweet citrus fruit famous for its use in marmalade and marinades.

Sofrito
Spanish tomato sauce adapted to the islands, used to enhance roasts and thicken stews or soups.

Soursop, Corossol, Guanábana
Elongated, spike-covered fruit, slightly tart and delicately flavored. It is used mainly in drinks, punches, sherbets and ice cream.

Sugar Apple, Sweetsop
Member of the cherimoya family, always served fresh.

Tamarind Puree
Highly acidic, sweet flavoring extracted from the pulp of tamarind pods. It is used in sauces, drinks and desserts.

West Indian Browning Sauce
Made from molasses and used to color and caramelize meat dishes.

Yam
Similar in size and color to the potato, but nuttier in flavor. It is not to be confused with the Southern sweet yam or sweet potato. Caribbean yams are served boiled, mashed or baked.

My first memory of sipping a planter's punch came shortly after I stepped from the bitter cold of New York into the steamy tropical heat of Guadeloupe. While we pasty-faced New Yorkers queued up to get through customs, a smiling hostess in a gaily patterned dress presented a trayful of hibiscus-pink drinks in plastic cups, a toast from the local chamber of commerce ensuring us a happy stay.

From classic rum punch to daiquiri, the Caribbean has produced some of the world's best-known drinks and cocktails. Almost every island has its own rum, and every local barman swears by his favorite rum recipe. Rum ranges in color from crystal clear to amber to the black of molasses, and its strength and subtlety can slide from firewater to mellow and smooth. Some aged rums can be sipped like fine cognac.

The ubiquitous daiquiri, a mix of white rum, sugar and lemon, took its name from a little mining town near Santiago, the old capital of Cuba. Invented by one of the foremen of the copper and nickel mines, it became a favorite of the U.S. miners who migrated there after the Spanish-American War and spent Saturday nights drinking at the bar of the venerable Venus Hotel.

Hemingway tasted his first daiquiri at the Floridita Bar in Havana, where he ordered doubles without sugar, known from then on among his adoring crowd as the "Pappa double." Over the years, this island trademark has been transformed, first into the frozen daiquiri and, more recently, into the frozen-fruit daiquiri, which replaces the lime juice with sweet bananas, pineapples, mangos or passion fruit. The all-American passion for strawberries has inspired its latest incarnation: the frozen strawberry daiquiri.

As with the daiquiri, the making of planter's punch depends on the ingenuity and whim of the barman, who decides if the rum is to be light or dark and whether the fruit juice of choice should be orange, pineapple, guava, mango or some unexpectedly eclectic combination.

Petit punch is my favorite apéritif in the French islands. Glass jars are filled to the brim with whatever fruit is ripe and in season—mango or guava, pineapple or passion fruit—sometimes spiced with fingers of ginger or a bunch of vanilla beans. Aged rum is then poured generously into the jars, and the lot is left to marinate for a couple of months.

For non-imbibers, there are natural fruit drinks as exotic as any cocktail: delicious concoctions of pawpaw, nutmeg, allspice and grapefruit juice; lychee nectar; fresh ginger beer; and refreshing infusions of hibiscus petals spiked with ginger, cloves and orange peel.

Trinidad Yellow Bird

Aromatic bitters, first produced in Port of Spain, is a distinctive additive to many island cocktails.

2 tablespoons Cointreau
2 tablespoons amber rum
1 teaspoon sugar syrup
Juice of ½ medium lime
Juice of 1 large orange
2 dashes Angostura bitters
Crushed ice

Pour all the drink ingredients into a cocktail shaker half-filled with crushed ice. Shake vigorously until the shaker begins to freeze. Strain into 2 chilled stemmed cocktail glasses.

Serves 2

Lychee Cocktail

This simply exotic cocktail is the Trinidadian martini.

½ cup canned lychee juice
¼ cup gin
½ cup dry vermouth
Crushed ice
2 lychees, for garnish

Mix drink ingredients with crushed ice in a blender or cocktail shaker. Divide between 2 glasses and serve with a lychee in each.

Serves 2

Watermelon & Lime Daiquiri

For a heady variation, cut a small hole in the melon and plug it with a bottle of rum. Left in the refrigerator for a day, the melon will absorb the alcohol. Slice into chunks, blend and serve.

4 cups watermelon, seeded and cut into 1-inch chunks
¼ cup fresh lime juice
¾ cup light rum
1 tablespoon plus 1 teaspoon sugar
Lime slices, for garnish

Place the watermelon chunks in a single layer in a large plastic bag. Freeze for 6 hours or overnight.

In a small bowl, combine the lime juice, rum and sugar; stir to dissolve the sugar. Pour the mixture into a blender. Add the frozen watermelon chunks and blend, breaking up any clumps, until smooth, about 1 minute. Pour into stemmed glasses and garnish each daiquiri with a slice of lime.

Serves 6

Coconut Refresher

Traditionally made without rum, this sweet-tart drink is a cooling delight on hot, lazy afternoons.

4 cups fresh Coconut Milk (page 139) or canned unsweetened
2 cups grapefruit juice
½ cup superfine sugar
2 tablespoons dark rum (optional)

Combine the ingredients and stir until the sugar dissolves. Serve in tall glasses over ice.

Serves 6

Pawpaw (Papaya) Cooler

This is digestive as well as delicious. A mango drink may be made similarly.

2 cups crushed or pureed ripe papaya
¾ cup plus 2 tablespoons superfine sugar
4 cups ice water
1 teaspoon grated fresh ginger
Juice of 1 or 2 medium limes
2 dashes Angostura bitters
Crushed ice

In a pitcher, combine the papaya, sugar and ice water. Stir until the sugar dissolves.

Stir in the ginger, lime juice to taste and the bitters. Serve in tall glasses over cracked ice.

Serves 4 to 6

Hibiscus Rum Punch

A Christmas tradition—made with the bright red hibiscus sepals that are called sorrel in the islands.

1 ounce fresh or dried hibiscus sepals
2 cups sugar
1 cinnamon stick
6 whole cloves
2 quarts boiling water
1 cup dark rum (optional)

In a heatproof jar or container, combine the hibiscus sepals, sugar, cinnamon stick and cloves. Pour on the boiling water and stir. Place a clean kitchen towel over the jar and set aside at room temperature for 2 to 3 days.

If adding rum, mix it in 2 days after making the mixture and allow the punch to stand for an additional 2 days.

Strain the mixture and pour into chilled tall glasses or over ice.

Serves 6 to 8

*G*uava Punch

Serve these in chilled tall glasses loaded with ice and lavishly decorated with chunks and slices of tropical fruit and—a true island must—the indispensable maraschino cherry.

2¼ cups unsweetened pineapple juice
2 cups guava juice, nectar or puree
¼ cup fresh lime juice
¾ cup medium-dark rum
4 dashes Angostura bitters

Mix all the ingredients and chill well. Serve on the rocks, dressed with tropical fruit.

Serves 5

*G*inger Beer

This tangy brew gets stronger the longer it is allowed to ferment.

4 to 6 ounces fresh ginger, peeled and minced
3½ cups sugar
4 cups boiling water
Grated zest and juice of 1 large lime

In a large glass bottle or earthenware jar, combine the ginger and sugar. Add the boiling water and stir until the sugar dissolves. Stir in the lime zest and juice. Set aside to cool. Cover and let stand for 5 to 6 days, stirring with a wooden spoon every day.

When fizzy, strain into clean glass bottles and chill. May be kept for 3 or more days.

Serves 8 to 10

Caribbean Fizz

This is a bubbly variation of the classic rum punch.

¼ cup light rum
1 cup sweet pineapple juice
1 tablespoon fresh lime juice
1 tablespoon superfine sugar
1 teaspoon Angostura bitters
Soda water

In a cocktail shaker, combine the rum, pineapple juice, lime juice, sugar and bitters, and shake well. Put ice cubes into 4 tall glasses and fill halfway with the mixture. Top with soda water and serve.

Serves 4

Jon & Sandra McClellan's Tobago Rum Punch

This recipe is the contemporary counterpart of the miniature lakes of punch that were served from rowboats at the lavish parties hosted by the sugarcane barons in years gone by.

Juice of 36 medium limes
6 cups sugar
3 cups water
½ cup Angostura bitters
1 cup maraschino cherries and their juice, pureed
About 1¼ bottles dark rum
About 1¼ bottles light rum
Freshly grated nutmeg
Crushed ice

In a nonreactive saucepan, boil the lime juice and sugar with the water for 10 minutes. Stir from time to time and cook until the sugar is completely dissolved. Cool.

Add the bitters and pureed cherries to the sugar syrup. Cover and refrigerate until cold.

To serve, pour 2 tablespoons of the syrup mixture, 2 tablespoons each dark and light rum and ground nutmeg to taste into each tall glass. Stir, add a straw and fill the glass with crushed ice. Serve. Or, combine syrup mixture, rums, and nutmeg to taste in a large punch bowl, and ladle into tall glasses filled with crushed ice.

Serves about 40

Piña Colada

This tropical crowd pleaser—a delight for summer entertaining—originated at Puerto Rico's La Barrachina Restaurant.

1 cup pineapple juice
½ cup cream of coconut
¼ cup heavy cream
½ cup amber rum
Cracked ice

Combine all of the liquid ingredients in a blender and fill with cracked ice. Blend well and pour into chilled goblets.

Serves 2

Island Coffee

This chilled espresso with a kick makes a delightful end to a Caribbean meal.

1 teaspoon superfine sugar
½ cup chilled espresso coffee
2 tablespoons Myers's rum or other dark, heavy rum
1 tablespoon Tia Maria liqueur
2 tablespoons heavy cream

Dissolve the sugar in the espresso and chill.

Pour the rum and Tia Maria into an 8-ounce stemmed glass and add the espresso mixture. Slowly pour the cream over the back of a teaspoon so the cream floats on top.

Serves 1

Each

noon hour, one feels the flurry of activity when resident islanders break from their daily work and escape to the nearest bar, restaurant or roadside shack to drink, eat and revive their spirits.

A West Indian lunch commences with the local drink of choice, often a daiquiri, rum punch or a beer. Before the meal proper, bite-size tidbits called *amuse-gueule* are set out on little plates to tempt the hungry and the gourmand alike.

In Guadeloupe and Martinique plates arrive piled high with creamy, spiced *boudin* bursting from their casings. The land crab's shell is filled with a stuffing of sweet crabmeat, aged rum and peppers, and the taste of cod fritters is dominated by the heat of bonnet peppers mixed with garlic and thyme. Jamaicans nibble on flaky curried meat or shrimp tarts—the curry underscoring the mix of spices that might include nutmeg, cinnamon and cloves. Barbadians and Trinidadians, on the other hand, have a special fondness for ''Pudn 'n souse''—the Bahamian classic of blood pudding and some pickled part of the pig. This ritual dish is a favorite for Saturday suppers, blow-out parties or Christmas morning celebrations.

No food exemplifies Caribbean cuisine better than salt cod, the thread that unifies cooking throughout the islands. From food shacks to the lean-tos on small highways and beaches, salt cod fritters appear under many guises. The Puerto Ricans and Spanish-speaking islands call them *bacalaitos*. They are known as *accra* in Trinidad, *stamp and go* in Jamaica, *acrats de morue* in the French islands and *calas* to the Dutch. Some are made with yeast or baking soda, others with flour, still others with mashed breadfruit or potato. Seasonings vary from island to island.

The omnipresent fritter can be based on hearts of palm, christophine, breadfruit, pumpkin or eggplant. In Jamaica, pea and bean fritters are favorites; the Trinidadian *phulouri* is a split-pea fritter; and on Dutch islands fritters are made of black-eyed peas.

In similar-name vein, most islands have the fried pastries stuffed with minced fish or meat called variously *pasteles, pastelitos, pastechis, empanadas, empanaditas* and *empanas*—all delights that prolong the cocktail hour until the cook decides that lunch is ready.

Stuffed Baked Plantains

These double-duty tidbits can be served with drinks or offered with a simple dinner of rice and beans.

4 ripe plantains
2 to 3 tablespoons unsalted butter, melted
4 bacon strips, cooked until crisp, chopped
1 teaspoon arrowroot
¼ cup fine, dry bread crumbs
1 tablespoon plus 1 teaspoon grated cheddar cheese

Preheat the oven to 400° F.

Peel the plantains and halve lengthwise. With a teaspoon, scoop out pulp from the middle of each plantain half, creating hollowed shells. Brush the shells with the melted butter.

In a medium bowl, mash the plantain pulp until smooth; fold in the bacon, arrowroot, bread crumbs and cheese. Fill the plantain shells with the mixture. Bake for 15 minutes and serve hot.

Serves 8

Féroce d'Avocat

This tangy treat accompanies prefatory rum drinks before the main meal. Barbadians serve a similar salt cod dish called *brule johl*.

8 ounces dried salt cod
½ cup white wine vinegar
1 small onion, finely chopped
1 garlic clove, crushed
6 scallions (including some of the green), chopped
1 fresh Scotch bonnet or other hot chili pepper, cored, seeded and minced
About ¼ cup peanut oil
1 large ripe avocado
Juice of 1 medium lime

Place the codfish in a nonreactive pot and cover with cold water. Add the vinegar; set aside overnight.

Prepare a charcoal fire or preheat the broiler. Remove the fish from the vinegar water and pat dry with a paper towel. When the coals burn with a dusty glow, char or broil the fish for 3 to 4 minutes on each side. When the fish is cool enough to handle, shred with a fork into fine bits.

In a medium bowl, mix the fish with the onion, garlic, scallions and chili pepper; bind together with the oil. Peel the avocado and mash the pulp into the mixture along with the lime juice.

Serve at room temperature by itself or with bread.

Serves 6 to 8

Fried Ripe Plantains

Plantains are to the Caribbean islands what the potato is stateside.

4 ripe plantains
3 to 4 tablespoons vegetable oil
Salt

Peel the plantains and cut crosswise in half. With a sharp paring knife, cut each half lengthwise into 4 slices.

Heat the oil in a large heavy skillet over medium heat. Fry the plantain slices on each side until golden. Drain on paper towels, season with salt and serve immediately.

Serves about 8

Piñones
PLANTAIN PINWHEELS

Ripe plantains can be sautéed in butter or baked, as in these little "wheels" of plantain strips wrapped in a tasty blend of spices and shellfish.

4 ripe plantains
16 medium shrimp, peeled and deveined
2 scallions (including some of the green), finely chopped
2 teaspoons dry sherry
1 teaspoon light soy sauce
1 teaspoon arrowroot
Cayenne pepper
Salt
2 teaspoons Oriental sesame oil

Preheat the oven to 375° F.

Cut the tips off and peel the plantains. Cut lengthwise into ⅛-inch slices (4 to 5 long slices).

With a sharp chopping knife, mince the shrimp to a paste. Place the paste in a bowl and fold in the scallions, sherry, soy sauce, arrowroot, cayenne and salt to taste.

Roll each plantain slice into a circle so that the ends overlap by at least 1 inch and secure with a toothpick. Fill the pinwheels with the paste.

Place the pinwheels on a baking sheet lightly coated with some of the sesame oil. Sprinkle with a little more cayenne and brush with the remaining sesame oil. Bake for 15 minutes.

Makes 16 to 20 pinwheels

Creole Clams

Serve with a loaf of French bread to mop up the sauce.

3 dozen littleneck clams, scrubbed
½ cup dry white wine
1 garlic clove, minced
8 scallions (including some of the green), finely chopped
½ fresh hot chili or Scotch bonnet pepper, seeded, deveined and finely chopped
Juice of 1 lemon
1 teaspoon chopped fresh chervil
1 teaspoon minced fresh parsley

Place the clams in the freezer for 10 minutes before cooking.

In a large nonreactive steamer, bring the wine to a boil over high heat. Add the clams and cook just until they open. Reserve the opened clams in a covered bowl; discard any that do not open.

Remove the steamer basket and toss in all of the remaining ingredients. Simmer for 1 minute. Pour the liquid over the clams and serve immediately.

Serves 4

Mero en Escabeche
PICKLED FISH

This dish may be served warm, but most Islanders prefer it marinated and chilled.

3 pounds snapper fillets, or other firm white fish
Salt
1½ cups olive oil
2 medium onions, thinly sliced
2 garlic cloves, minced
2 bay leaves
¼ teaspoon black peppercorns, crushed
1 large tomato, peeled, seeded and chopped
¾ cup fresh lime juice
¾ cup small pimiento-stuffed green olives
2 tablespoons capers, drained

Cut the fillets into 1½-inch pieces and season with salt.

In a large nonreactive skillet, heat 3 tablespoons of the olive oil. Fry the fish on each side until lightly browned.

Place the fillets in a nonreactive bowl.

Add 2 tablespoons of oil to the skillet, and add the onions, garlic, bay leaves and peppercorns. Sauté for 8 minutes, or until the onions are tender. Set aside to cool.

When cool, add the remaining olive oil, chopped tomato, lime juice, stuffed green olives and capers to the onion mixture. Pour over the fillets, cover and refrigerate for 24 hours.

Serve cold.

Serves 6 to 8

Stuffed Crab Backs

Island crabs live in the mud just above the sandy beaches and are just as sweet and tender as their American cousins.

½ cup Light Fish Stock (page 107)
2 tablespoons hot chili sauce
4 scallions (including some of the green), trimmed and coarsely chopped
10 green olives, pitted
2 tablespoons capers, drained
½ cup fresh coriander leaves
½ cup parsley leaves
Salt
1 pound lump crabmeat, picked clean
2 eggs, lightly beaten
2 tablespoons fresh lemon juice
½ cup dry bread crumbs
6 washed crab shells (optional)
8 tablespoons (1 stick) unsalted butter

In a food processor, combine the stock chili sauce, scallions, olives, capers, coriander, parsley, and salt to taste. Pulse for 20 seconds.

Transfer the mixture to a large bowl and fold in the crabmeat. Add the eggs and the fresh lemon juice, and then mix thoroughly.

Stuff the crab shells or small ramekins with the mixture, or form the mixture into 8 to 10 small cakes, each about 2 inches in diameter. Cover and refrigerate for 30 minutes.

Coat the stuffed crabs or cakes with the bread crumbs. Refrigerate for 20 minutes.

Preheat the oven to 300° F.

Place 1 teaspoon of the butter on top of each stuffed crab or crab cake. Liberally coat a baking sheet with the remaining butter. Place the stuffed crabs or cakes on the sheet and bake for 15 to 20 minutes, or until golden.

Serve immediately with hot sauce and Mango Chutney (page 134).

Serves 6

Note: This recipe may be used for fried crab cakes. Melt the butter in a skillet, add the chilled crab cakes and fry until golden on each side.

heart of Palm Fritters

All islands have variations on the fritter, and this recipe offers more Gallic know-how than most.

1 pound fresh palm heart, or 1 can
   (16 ounces) hearts of palm, drained
Juice of ½ large lime
1 cup all-purpose flour
1 teaspoon baking powder
1 teaspoon salt
2 eggs, lightly beaten
1 medium onion, finely chopped
2 garlic cloves, minced
2 Scotch bonnet or other hot chili
   peppers, seeded, deveined and
   minced
1 tablespoon chopped parsley
½ teaspoon chopped fresh thyme
1 tablespoon chopped chives
Freshly ground black pepper
About 4 tablespoons milk
Vegetable oil, for frying

If using fresh palm heart, peel off the outside layer. Cut the flesh into 1-inch-thick rounds. Slice lengthwise into thin strips. Sprinkle with the lime juice and reserve.

In a large mixing bowl, sift the flour, baking powder and salt. Whisk in the eggs, onion, garlic, chili peppers, parsley, thyme, chives, and pepper to taste. Add the milk, 1 tablespoonful at a time, to lighten the mixture. Fold in the palm. Cover and set aside.

In a deep-fryer, heat the oil to 375° F. Drop the mixture by tablespoonfuls into the hot oil and fry until golden. Remove the fritters with a slotted spoon and drain on paper towels. Continue frying in small batches until all of the fritters are cooked. Serve hot with Sauce Chien (page 138) or hot sauce.

Makes about 14 fritters; serves 4 to 5

acrats de Morue

COD FRITTERS

These golden-fried nuggets—a must before any French Caribbean meal—are as habit-forming as a bowl of peanuts.

1 pound salt cod, soaked overnight, drained and flaked
1 Scotch bonnet or other fresh hot chili pepper, minced
1 garlic clove, minced
1 medium onion, finely chopped
1 medium bunch chives, finely chopped
½ teaspoon minced fresh thyme
2 cups all-purpose flour
1 cup water
1 tablespoon baking powder
Salt and white pepper
2 egg whites
4 cups vegetable oil, for frying

In a large mixing bowl, mix the cod with the vegetables and herbs; set aside.

In a medium bowl, mix the flour and water to make a loose paste. Add the baking powder and season with salt and pepper. Fold in the cod mixture.

In a small bowl, beat the egg whites until stiff and glossy. Fold one-third of the whites into the cod mixture to lighten it. Fold in the remaining whites.

In a deep, heavy pot, heat the oil over medium-high heat until it reaches 350° F. Using an oval tablespoon, drop spoonfuls of the mixture into the hot oil and fry until golden brown. Drain on paper towels. Continue frying in batches until all of the batter is used.

Serve immediately with Sauce Chien (page 138).

Serves 6

Eggplant Fritters

The whole Caribbean basin uses all sorts of vegetables to make fritters. This is a French-island favorite.

2 medium eggplants (about 1½ pounds)
Salt
1 egg
2 tablespoons milk
1 tablespoon finely chopped parsley
Freshly ground black pepper
1 cup all-purpose flour
1 teaspoon baking powder
Vegetable oil, for frying

Peel the eggplants and cut into 1-inch cubes. Salt the cubes liberally and drain in a colander for 30 minutes.

In a large pot of boiling water, cook the eggplant cubes for 10 to 15 minutes, or until tender. Drain and cool.

Place the eggplant in a food processor and pulse on and off until pureed. Place the puree into a large bowl and whisk in the egg, milk, parsley, and pepper to taste. Sift the flour and baking powder into the mixture and blend; reserve.

In a deep-fryer, heat the oil to 375° F. Drop the mixture by tablespoonfuls into the oil and fry until golden. Remove the fritters with a slotted spoon and drain on paper towels. Continue frying in small batches until all the fritters are cooked.

Serve hot with Sauce Chien (page 138) or hot sauce.

Serves 4 to 6

Brule Johl

This salad is served in a halved avocado shell or on salad greens and, in the English-speaking islands, with ship's biscuits, a.k.a. hardtack.

1 pound dried salt cod
1 small onion, chopped
2 medium tomatoes, peeled, seeded and chopped
2 tablespoons olive oil
Juice of 2 limes plus 1 tablespoon
1 bell pepper, cored, seeded and finely chopped
1 hot red chili pepper, cored, seeded and minced
1 small ripe avocado, halved, pitted and diced
1 head of Bibb lettuce

Soak the fish in cold water and refrigerate overnight. Pat the fish dry with paper towels. Clean and finely shred the fish.

In a large bowl, combine the fish, onion, tomatoes, oil, the juice of 2 limes, the bell pepper and chili pepper. Mix well; refrigerate until chilled.

Toss the avocado with the remaining 1 tablespoon of lime juice. Arrange the lettuce on 4 chilled plates. Divide the brule johl among them. Sprinkle with the diced avocado and serve.

Serves 4

Souse

This traditional dish is served with blood pudding for Sunday lunch, and always at holiday time. Blood pudding is sold at West Indian markets and some Spanish markets, where it is called *morcilla*.

2 pounds lean pork, cubed
2 pig's trotters (pig's feet)
About ¼ cup salt
2 cups fresh lime juice
4 shallots, minced
2 Scotch bonnet or other hot chili peppers, seeded, deveined and minced

In a large nonreactive pot, combine the pork, pig's trotters, salt, and enough water to cover. Bring to a boil over high heat. Skim, reduce the heat to a simmer and cook until the meat cubes are fork-tender and the skin begins to pull away from the trotters, about 1 hour. Drain and cool under cold running water. Drain thoroughly and set aside to cool completely.

In a large bowl, mix the lime juice with the shallots, chili pepper, 1 cup of water, and salt to taste. Set aside.

Pick the meat off the trotters and shred or chop the cubed meat pieces. Toss the meat with the lime juice mixture. Cover and refrigerate for 8 hours, or overnight.

Drain the souse and serve chilled, with a Caribbean hot sauce or Pepper Wine (page 139) and blood pudding.

Serves 6 or more

Achards

This is island chowchow—any vegetable mélange will do. Fresh heart of palm is available in many gourmet shops.

½ small green cabbage, cored and
    shredded
1 small cauliflower, trimmed and broken
    into florets
8 ounces fresh palm heart, trimmed, soft
    flesh cut into ½-inch disks
8 ounces string beans, trimmed and cut
    into 1-inch lengths
2 large carrots, peeled, cut into 1-inch
    rounds and quartered
Salt
4 tablespoons olive oil
1 medium onion, finely chopped
1 fresh hot red chili pepper, peeled,
    deveined and minced
1 garlic clove, minced
2 to 3 pinches saffron
Freshly ground black pepper
1 cup white wine vinegar

Place the cabbage, cauliflower, heart of palm, beans and carrots into separate containers. Add salt to taste to each and cover with cold water. Refrigerate for 24 hours.

Coat a medium skillet with 1 tablespoon of the oil. Add the onion and wilt over medium heat. Add the chili pepper and garlic, and cook for 10 minutes, or until wilted. Fold in the saffron and season with ground pepper to taste. Add the vinegar and the remaining 3 tablespoons oil; reserve.

Bring a large kettle of lightly salted water to a boil. Drain the vegetables; plunge each into the boiling water for 1 minute. Rinse under cold running water and drain thoroughly.

Mix the vegetables with the onion vinaigrette mixture and refrigerate until cold. Arrange on a platter and serve.

Serves 6 or more

ξmpanada de Pollo
CHICKEN PIE

This chicken pie dances with Spanish flavor. It provides a pleasant luncheon dish along with a salad.

PASTRY
4 cups all-purpose flour
½ teaspoon baking powder
1 teaspoon salt
12 tablespoons (1½ sticks) unsalted butter, chilled and cut into small bits
1 egg
About ½ cup ice-cold water

FILLING
5 pounds cut-up chicken pieces
Juice of 1 lime
Salt and freshly ground pepper
2 tablespoons olive oil
2 medium onions, finely chopped
1 medium green bell pepper, seeded, deveined and finely chopped
1 medium red bell pepper, seeded, deveined and finely chopped
4 medium ripe tomatoes, peeled, seeded and chopped; or 2 cups canned plum tomatoes
½ cup red wine
1 teaspoon cayenne pepper
1 tablespoon fresh oregano, or 1 teaspoon dried
1 teaspoon fresh thyme, or ½ teaspoon dried
1 bay leaf
¼ cup chopped pimiento-stuffed green olives
2 teaspoons capers, drained and chopped
1 egg yolk
1 tablespoon ice water

To make the pastry: In the bowl of an electric mixer, sift the flour with the baking powder and salt. Add the butter and mix at the lowest speed until the mixture is the consistency of cornmeal. Add the egg, increase the speed and gradually add the ice water, 1 tablespoon at a time until the pastry pulls away from the sides and adheres to the beater.

Remove the pastry to a lightly floured surface and divide in half. Cover with wax paper and refrigerate for 45 minutes before rolling out.

To make the filling: In a shallow dish, coat the chicken pieces with the lime juice and season with salt and pepper.

In a heavy nonreactive skillet, heat the oil over medium heat. Add the chicken and sauté until golden on all sides. Remove and set aside.

Add the onions and bell peppers to the skillet, and sauté until the onions are translucent, about 8 minutes.

Add the tomatoes, wine, cayenne, oregano, thyme and bay leaf to the skillet, and simmer for 15 minutes. Return the chicken pieces to the pan, cover and simmer for 30 minutes, or until the chicken is tender.

Remove the chicken from the sauce and set aside. When cool enough to handle, remove the skin and bones from the chicken and coarsely chop the meat.

Over medium heat, bring the sauce to a simmer and continue cooking until the sauce is thickened, about 10 minutes. Remove the bay leaf and add the olives, capers and chicken. Set aside.

Preheat the oven to 350° F.

On a lightly floured surface, roll out half of the pastry to fit a 7 x 12-inch rectangular baking dish. Line the dish, allowing the pastry to overlap the edges. Add the chicken mixture.

Roll out the remaining pastry. Lightly beat the egg yolk with the ice water and moisten the edges of the pastry shell with the egg wash. Cover with the pastry and seal the edges. With a paring knife, cut 4 to 6 slits in the surface of the pastry. Brush the surface with the remaining egg wash and bake for 45 minutes, or until the crust is golden.

Cut into squares and serve hot or cold.

Serves 8 to 10

Avocados with Bacon & Shrimp

This recipe makes a luxurious first-course dipping sauce for cold shrimp or vegetables and is equally good served on toast.

6 bacon slices, finely chopped
1 small onion, finely chopped
4 large shrimp, peeled, deveined and
**   chopped**
2 teaspoons chopped fresh coriander
**   leaves**
2 medium avocados (each about
**   10 ounces)**
2 teaspoons fresh lime juice
Freshly ground black pepper
4 lime wedges

In a small skillet, render the bacon over medium heat until golden. Remove and drain on paper towels. Add the onion to the bacon fat and sauté until wilted but not browned. Add the chopped shrimp and cook for 2 minutes. Fold in the bacon and coriander; remove from the heat and set aside to cool.

Halve the avocados, remove the pits and scoop out the flesh; reserve the avocado shells. Place the avocado pulp in a small mixing bowl, add the lime juice and pepper, and whisk until smooth. Fold in the bacon and shrimp mixture and taste for seasoning.

Fill the avocado shells with the mixture, garnish with the lime wedges and serve immediately.

Serves 4

Jamaican Beef Patties

Patties are a universal snack food in Jamaica and elsewhere—and there are countless variations throughout the Caribbean islands.

FILLING
3 tablespoons vegetable oil
1½ pounds lean beef, ground
1 medium onion, finely chopped
3 garlic cloves, minced
1 fresh hot chili pepper, seeded and minced
3 scallions (including some of the green), minced
1 tablespoon curry powder
½ teaspoon ground cumin
1 tablespoon dried thyme
Salt and freshly ground pepper
½ cup coarse, dry bread crumbs
½ cup fresh or canned beef or chicken stock

PASTRY
1½ cups all-purpose flour
1 teaspoon curry powder
¼ teaspoon salt
10 tablespoons (1¼ sticks) unsalted butter or margarine, cut into bits
¼ cup ice water

To make the filling: In a medium skillet, heat the oil over medium heat. Add the beef, onion, garlic, chili pepper and scallions; sauté, stirring constantly, until the mixture gives off its moisture, about 8 minutes. Add the remaining filling ingredients and simmer, stirring often, for 20 minutes. The filling should be moist but not wet. Set aside to cool.

To make the pastry: Sift the flour, curry powder and salt into a large mixing bowl. Mix in the butter and rub with your fingers until it is the consistency of cornmeal. Add the ice water, 1 tablespoon at a time, until the dough just holds together. Cover; refrigerate for 1 hour.

Preheat the oven to 400° F.

On a lightly floured board, roll out the pastry about ⅛ inch thick. Using a 4-inch round cookie cutter, cut the pastry into disks. Place 1 tablespoon of the filling slightly below the center of each round. Fold over the pastry to form a half-moon and seal the edges with the tines of a fork. Place the patties on a lightly greased baking sheet. Bake for 30 minutes, or until golden brown.

Serves 4 to 6

Stamp & Go

Small food stands are set up at bus stops all over Jamaica. Passengers bounce off the bus to grab a couple of these treats, and then hop back on—hence the local lingo "stamp and go."

4 ounces dried salt cod
½ cup sifted all-purpose flour
½ teaspoon baking powder
1 egg, lightly beaten
2 to 3 tablespoons ice water
1 medium onion, minced
1 garlic clove, minced
½ Scotch bonnet or other hot chili pepper, minced
½ teaspoon chopped fresh thyme, or ¼ teaspoon dried salt
Vegetable oil, for frying

Soak the fish in cold water and refrigerate overnight. On the next day, clean and finely shred the fish; set aside.

In a large bowl, mix the fish, flour, baking powder, beaten egg and just enough of the ice water to thin out the batter. Mix in the onion, garlic, chili pepper, thyme, and salt to taste. Set aside.

In a deep-fryer, heat the oil to 375° F. Drop the mixture by tablespoonfuls into the oil and fry until golden. Remove the fritters with a slotted spoon and drain on paper towels. Continue frying in small batches until all the fritters are cooked.

Served hot, with Caribbean hot sauce.

Serves 6

Lauretta's Tropical Salad

The French-speaking islands all serve smoked fish—smoked kingfish is a delicacy on the island of Les Saints, and smoked eels are popular in Martinique. This exotic combination is the creative handiwork of a Martiniquaise friend.

¼ cup good-quality red wine vinegar
1 teaspoon dry mustard
1 teaspoon Dijon mustard
Salt and freshly ground pepper
¾ cup olive oil
2 heads ruby red butter crunch lettuce, washed and dried
1 pound smoked eel, skinned, boned and cut into 1½-inch lengths
1 pickled red chili pepper, seeded and diced
1 ugli fruit or pink grapefruit, peeled, pith removed and cut into sections
1 avocado, peeled, pitted and diced

In a bowl, whisk together the vinegar and the seasonings; mix thoroughly, until the salt dissolves. Gradually whisk in the oil until emulsified.

In a large chilled bowl, combine the lettuce, eel, chili pepper, fruit and avocado. Add enough of the dressing to coat lightly.

Toss and serve.

Serves 4

Soups And Stews

The

very heart of Caribbean cuisine is one-pot cooking—best expressed in soups and stews, the backbone of all great peasant fare.

No stew in the English-speaking islands begins without the buying of "a bunch of sive"—spring onions or scallions tied in a bouquet with parsley and a sprig of thyme—to toss into the pot. The French-speaking islands tie together their "bouquet garni" of scallions, parsley and thyme with perhaps a carrot and an occasional leek. The Spanish-speaking islands include some of the same herbs, but many of their dishes start with *sofrito*—a base made from onions, garlic, tomato, green peppers and hot chili peppers that lends flavor and body. Ham bones, slab bacon and lard, as well as chorizo sausage, flavor the soups and stews Cubans call *potages*—along with other Iberian staples like olive oil, saffron and the American tomato.

Pepperpot is a traditional dish served in Jamaica and other English-speaking islands. When a soup, it includes a cornucopia of vegetables. When a stew, it calls for any combination of beef, pork, chicken and oxtail. Pepperpot has one ingredient that gives it a unique taste: the Amerindian contribution of cassareep, a bittersweet sauce made from grated cassava root and found in West Indian markets. The effect can be just as good when slightly burned caramelized sugar is used instead.

Callaloo, a large leafy vegetable, tastes like a combination of spinach and kale. It makes a marvelous soup—rich in stock, as green as the sea.

Jigote, a lavish chicken soup laced with sherry and a quenelle-like chicken liver and meat dumpling; *sopa de frijol negro,* the velvety black bean soup, spiked with cumin and hot chili pepper from Cuba; *soupe au poisson,* redolent of bay rum berries, saffron, ginger, capers and chunks of pearly-white fish from Martinique and Guadeloupe; and the pigeon pea soup from Puerto Rico, dense with pieces of West Indian pumpkin and pork sausage are characteristic of the lusty home-style soup meals typical of island cooking.

Casseroles of rabbit, chicken and turkey are sparked with any combination of rum, bitter orange, and an abundance of savory herbs, and are always chockful of garden-fresh vegetables. The cook completes the jazz pot with his or her own interpretation of the quantity of chili peppers used.

Soup or stew, these meals-in-one are accompanied by boiled white rice, beans and twice-fried plantains—with hot crusty bread to sop up the juices.

Just as the cold salads, meats and fish served in Nordic countries tend to warm the blood, the array of hot dishes presented in the Caribbean will cool it—with a vengeance.

Sopa de Frijol Negro
BLACK BEAN SOUP

Some Cuban cooks float a slice of lemon or a bit of the chopped white and yolk of a hard-cooked egg on this velvety brown-black soup. Chunks of cooked lobster are another inspired addition.

2 cups dried black beans, soaked
   overnight
8 to 10 cups fresh or canned chicken stock
3 tablespoons olive oil
1 medium onion, chopped
2 garlic cloves, chopped
1 cup Sofrito (page 137)
½ teaspoon ground cumin
1 medium potato, peeled and grated
Salt and freshly ground pepper
Dark rum or Pepper Wine (page 139)

Drain the beans thoroughly and transfer the beans to a large stockpot. Add enough stock to cover the beans by about 2 inches. Bring to a boil, reduce the heat, cover and simmer for 1 hour.

Stir from time to time, making sure that the beans do not stick to the bottom of the pot.

In a nonreactive skillet, heat the olive oil and sauté the onion and garlic for 8 minutes, or until the onion is tender. Add the Sofrito and cumin to the onion mixture and blend. Add the onion mixture and grated potato to the beans and cook for 45 minutes, or until the beans are tender.

Drain the cooked beans, reserving the liquid. In a food processor, puree the beans with some of the liquid until smooth, about 2 cups at a time.

Return the beans and the bean liquid to the pot; add salt and pepper to taste. Simmer for 15 minutes.

Serve in heated soup plates with a teaspoon of dark rum or a dash or two of Pepper Wine.

Serves 6 to 8

Green Pigeon Pea Soup

Pea-based soups are more often than not served with chunks of ham or sausage. The Dutch slice frankfurters, and the Spanish use longaniza or chorizo.

1 pound chorizo or longaniza sausage
2 tablespoons olive oil
1 medium onion, minced
2 garlic cloves, chopped
1 pound fresh or canned green pigeon
    peas (*gandules*)
5 cups fresh or canned chicken stock
1 cup fresh Coconut Milk (page 139) or
    canned unsweetened
8 ounces calabaza (West Indian pumpkin)
    or winter squash, peeled and cut into
    1-inch cubes
1 cup Sofrito (page 137)
1 coriander sprig
Salt and freshly ground pepper

In a large nonreactive saucepan, cook the sausage until lightly browned and most of the fat is rendered. Remove the sausage and pour off the excess fat. Add the olive oil, onion and garlic, and cook until the onion is translucent.

Add the pigeon peas, stock, coconut milk, calabaza, Sofrito, coriander, and salt and pepper to taste. Cover and simmer until the pigeon peas and pumpkin are tender and the soup thickens, about 30 minutes.

Slice the sausage into ½-inch rounds, add to the soup and continue to cook for another 5 minutes, or until the sausages are heated through.

Serve in heated bowls with boiled white rice and hot sauce or Pepper Wine (page 139).

Serves 6

Cold Avocado Soup

Avocados grow like apples in the Caribbean. They are rich, nourishing—and fattening.

2 tablespoons unsalted butter
3 shallots, minced
1 tablespoon grated fresh ginger
2 large ripe avocados, peeled and pitted
Juice of 1 lime
3 cups fresh or canned chicken stock
½ teaspoon cayenne pepper
Salt and freshly ground pepper
1 cup light cream
Chopped fresh chives

In a nonreactive stockpot, melt the butter over medium heat. Add the shallots and ginger and sauté for 2 minutes.

In a small bowl, mash the avocados with the lime juice. Add to the shallot mixture along with the stock, cayenne, and salt and pepper to taste. Whisk the soup to remove any lumps and simmer for 10 minutes. Refrigerate until chilled.

When ready to serve, whisk in the cream. Serve in chilled bowls and sprinkle with chopped chives.

Serves 5 to 6

Jigote
RICH CHICKEN CONSOMMÉ

The Cuban version of Mama's chicken soup is a rich and comforting elixir.

4 pounds chicken pieces with giblets and liver reserved
3 pounds beef shin, rump or chuck
2 large veal bones
3 carrots, washed and roughly chopped
3 celery ribs with leaves, roughly chopped
2 large onions, peeled and cut in half
2 large tomatoes, cut in half
2 garlic cloves
2 bay leaves, crushed
12 peppercorns
2 sprigs fresh thyme, or 1 teaspoon dried
2 sprigs fresh marjoram, or 1 teaspoon dried
6 parsley sprigs
1 small bunch chives
1 cup dry sherry
Salt and freshly ground pepper
Angostura bitters
Snipped chives

Rinse the chicken pieces, beef and veal bones under cold running water, and place them in a large stockpot. Add enough cold water to cover by 2 inches. Add the carrots, celery, onions, tomatoes, garlic, bay leaves, peppercorns and herbs, and bring to a boil over high heat. Skim the surface, reduce the heat and simmer for 2½ to 3 hours, or until the meats are fork-tender. Add the reserved giblets and liver and simmer for an additional 15 minutes, or until the giblets are tender. Remove the giblets and the meats and veal bones from the stock and set aside to cool. Continue simmering the soup for 1½ hours, or until the soup is reduced to 3 quarts.

Line a strainer with a double thickness of dampened cheesecloth and strain the stock. Discard the solids. Cover and refrigerate until thoroughly chilled or overnight.

When the meats are cool, remove the white meat from one of the chicken breast halves; reserve the remaining chicken for another use. Shred enough of the meat from the beef and veal bones to measure about 1 generous cup. Cover and refrigerate the chicken and meats.

When the stock is chilled, skim off the fat and place the soup in a large stockpot over medium heat. Add the sherry and bring to a simmer. Cook for 15 minutes, or until the soup is hot. Season with salt and pepper to taste.

In a food processor, puree the reserved chicken breast, the shredded meat, gizzard and liver. Taste and season with salt and pepper.

Place 1 teaspoon of the puree in each heated bowl and ladle in the hot soup.

Serve with a dash of bitters and snipped chives.

Serves 12

Sopa de Camarones
SHRIMP SOUP

Shrimp soup is popular throughout the Spanish-speaking islands and, when bolstered by a green salad, cheese and fruit, makes a satisfying lunch.

1 pound medium shrimp
3 tablespoons olive oil
1 cup white wine
1 cup water
1 medium onion, finely chopped
1 garlic clove, minced
1 green bell pepper, seeded and diced
3 large tomatoes, peeled, seeded and
    coarsely chopped
1 bay leaf, crushed
¼ teaspoon ground cumin
4 ears sweet corn, kernels cut off, cobs
    scraped and reserved, or 8 ounces
    frozen corn kernels
6 new potatoes, peeled and halved
4 cups homemade or canned chicken
    stock
Salt and pepper
2 tablespoons lime juice

Peel the shrimp and reserve the shells.
  In a large nonreactive skillet, heat 1 tablespoon of the oil over medium heat. Add the shrimp shells and sauté for 3 minutes, or until the shells become red and give off their flavor. Add the wine and water, bring to a boil and cook until reduced by half. Strain the shells and discard them, reserving the shrimp stock.

Add the remaining 2 tablespoons oil to the skillet. Add the onion, garlic and bell pepper and sauté for 10 minutes, or until the vegetables are tender. Add the tomatoes, bay leaf, cumin, corn cobs and shrimp stock. Cover and cook for 15 minutes.

Add the potatoes and chicken stock, and cover and simmer for another 15 minutes, or until the potatoes are tender. Remove the corn cobs and add the shrimp and reserved corn kernels, and cook an additional 5 minutes. Season with salt and pepper and add the lime juice.

Serve in heated bowls with boiled white rice and beans.

Serves 4 as a main course

Callaloo & Crab

This unusual winner is one of the Caribbean's many gastronomic treats. Spinach, Swiss chard or kale come close to the original flavor of callaloo and substitute nicely for it.

3 pounds fresh callaloo, or spinach, Swiss
    chard or kale, stems removed; or
    2 pounds swiss chard mixed with
    1 pound spinach
8 ounces fresh okra, stems removed, cut
    into ¼-inch rounds
About 6 cups fresh or canned chicken
    stock
¼ cup vegetable oil
4 ounces salt pork, cut into ¼-inch dice;
    or 1 smoked pig's tail, diced
1 medium onion, chopped
1 garlic clove, chopped
6 scallions (including some of the green),
    chopped
1 Scotch bonnet or other fresh hot chili
    pepper, seeded and finely chopped
1 pound fresh lump crabmeat, picked
    clean
Juice of 1 lime
1 cup fresh Coconut Milk (page 139) or
    canned unsweetened
2 thyme sprigs
Salt and freshly ground pepper

Rinse the callaloo (or substitute) and okra thoroughly in cold water and drain.

In a large nonreactive soup kettle, add the callaloo and okra and enough stock to cover. Bring to a boil over high heat. Drain, reserving the greens, okra and cooking liquid.

Heat the oil in a large nonreactive saucepan. Add the salt pork or pig's tail and sauté until golden. Remove from the pan and drain on paper towels. Add the onion and garlic, and sauté until lightly browned. Stir in the scallions and chili pepper, and sauté for another 2 minutes. Stir in the crabmeat and lime juice, and blend well. Set aside.

Puree the greens and okra in a food processor, adding a little of the reserved cooking liquid to keep the mixture lightly soupy. Pour the puree into a clean nonreactive saucepan and set over medium heat. Add the pork and crabmeat mixture. Stir in the coconut milk and thyme sprigs. Season with salt and freshly ground pepper to taste.

Add 2 cups of the reserved cooking liquid, or enough of the liquid to keep the mixture thick and soupy. Bring to a boil. Reduce the heat and simmer for 10 minutes.

Serve immediately in heated bowls with boiled white rice and Banane Pésé (page 129).

Serves 6 to 8

Soupe au Poisson

Cooks in Guadeloupe add a dash of Ricard, an anise-flavored spirit similar to Pernod, to this classic French dish. The Martinique cook serves the soup with toasted garlic croutons and grated Gruyère cheese.

4 tablespoons olive oil
2 medium onions, chopped
4 scallions (including some of the green), chopped
1 thyme sprig
10 cups cold water
3 pounds cleaned firm white fish (such as snapper, grouper or bass), head, tail and spine reserved and gills removed
3 garlic cloves, crushed
3 bay rum berries, or 2 allspice berries
1 bay rum leaf or bay leaf
2 whole Scotch bonnet or other fresh hot chili peppers
1 pound new potatoes, peeled and cut into 1-inch cubes
1 pound ripe tomatoes, peeled, seeded and chopped
1/8 teaspoon saffron, crumbled
1 tablespoon Ricard
2 tablespoons drained capers
1/4 cup fresh basil julienne, or 1/4 cup minced fresh parsley

Heat the oil in a large nonreactive stockpot or saucepan. Add the onions, scallions and thyme, and sauté until translucent. Add the water, the fish head, tail and spine, the garlic, spices and peppers. Bring to a boil. Reduce to a simmer and cook, uncovered, for 30 minutes.

Remove the peppers from the stock and discard. Line a strainer with a double layer of dampened cheesecloth and strain the soup through a fine sieve, pressing lightly to extract the juices. Discard the solids.

Return the stock to a clean saucepan and add the potatoes. Simmer for 10 minutes, or until the potatoes are almost cooked. Add the tomatoes and saffron.

Cut the fish fillets into 2-inch cubes. Add to the stock and simmer for 8 minutes, or until the fish is opaque.

Add the Ricard and capers, and simmer for 5 minutes.

Serve in heated bowls and sprinkle with the basil. Accompany the soup with toasted garlic croutons and grated Gruyère cheese.

Serves 6 to 8

Blaff

The island word *blaff* duplicates the sound of the fish hitting the broth—and provides the perfect name for this signature dish.

4 cups Light Fish Stock (page 107)
1 cup dry white wine
6 scallions (including some of the green), chopped
1 garlic clove, crushed
2 whole cloves
1 whole Scotch bonnet or other fresh hot chili pepper
2 bay rum berries or allspice berries
2 bay rum leaves, or 1 bay leaf
½ teaspoon fresh thyme
4 small red snapper fillets (about 2 pounds) or other firm white-fleshed fish fillets such as black bass or grouper, with skin intact
1 teaspoon finely chopped fresh parsley
2 limes, cut in half

In a deep nonreactive saucepan, combine the stock, wine, scallions, garlic, cloves, chili peppers, rum berries, rum leaves and thyme. Bring to a boil. Reduce the heat and simmer for 15 minutes.

Add the fish and poach at a simmer for about 8 minutes, or until opaque.

Place 1 fillet in each of 4 warm shallow plates.

Strain the broth into a nonreactive saucepan. Add the parsley and bring to a simmer. Spoon the liquid over the fish.

Serve with boiled white rice and lime halves to squeeze into the soup.

Serves 4

Curried Lobster Soup

Island lobsters are always a treat. This recipe calls for only one but feeds four lobster lovers.

3 tablespoons unsalted butter
3 shallots, minced
1 celery rib, minced
1 tablespoon curry powder
1 medium tomato, peeled, seeded and chopped
2 cups Light Fish Stock (page 107)
1 cup heavy cream
1 pound uncooked shelled lobster meat, chopped
Salt and freshly ground pepper
Juice of ½ lime
Freshly grated nutmeg
2 tablespoons minced parsley

In a large nonreactive stockpot, melt the butter over medium heat. Add the shallots and celery and sauté until the vegetables sweat out their juices. Add the curry powder and cook, stirring constantly, for 1 minute. Add the tomato and cook for 1 more minute. Add the stock and bring to a simmer. Cook for 10 minutes.

Meanwhile, scald the cream over medium heat. Add the lobster and hot cream to the soup mixture. Season with salt and pepper and add the lime juice and a few gratings of nutmeg. Cook for about 2 minutes, or until the lobster meat is pink and slightly firm.

Serve in warm soup plates and sprinkle with the parsley.

Serves 4 to 5

Asopao de Pollo
CHICKEN & RICE STEW

Asopaos are delicious soupy stews that demand warm bread for mopping up.

2 tablespoons fresh oregano, or
    1 tablespoon dried
1 tablespoon fresh thyme, or
    2 teaspoons dried
4 garlic cloves, chopped
Salt
6 pounds cut-up chicken pieces
3 tablespoons olive oil
2 medium onions, finely chopped
2 medium green bell peppers, seeded and
    chopped
4 medium tomatoes, peeled, seeded and
    chopped; or 2 cups canned plum
    tomatoes
2 cups long-grain white rice
5 cups fresh or canned chicken stock
1 cup dry white wine
Freshly ground black pepper
1 cup fresh or frozen cooked green peas
2 tablespoons capers, drained
¼ cup pitted green olives
3 pimientos, cut into strips

In a small bowl, mix the oregano, thyme, garlic, and salt to taste. Coat the chicken pieces thoroughly with the mixture. Set the chicken aside.

In a large nonreactive heavy skillet, heat the oil over medium heat and sauté the chicken, a few pieces at a time, until golden on all sides. Set aside.

Add the onion and bell pepper to the skillet and cook until the onion is translucent, about 10 minutes. Add the tomatoes and simmer for 5 minutes.

Add the chicken to the skillet, cover and cook over low heat for 30 minutes, or until the chicken pieces are fork-tender. Remove the chicken pieces and set aside to cool.

Add the rice, stock, wine, and freshly ground pepper to taste to the skillet. Cover and cook over low heat until the rice is tender, about 20 minutes.

Remove and discard the skin and bones from the chicken. Shred the chicken and add it to the rice mixture. Fold in the peas, capers, olives and pimiento strips. Cover and simmer 10 minutes, or until the chicken is heated through. The dish should be soupy.

Serves 6

Jamaican Pepperpot

The important ingredient here is cassareep, a black syrup made from cassava root, which is considered a tenderizer as well as a preservative.

2 teaspoons West Indian browning sauce
1 pound oxtail, cut into 1-inch pieces
2 pounds lean boneless pork or beef, cut into 1-inch cubes
4 pounds cut-up chicken pieces
8 ounces salt beef, diced
½ cup cassareep
2 medium onions, sliced
6 garlic cloves, chopped
4 fresh hot red chili peppers, cored, seeded and chopped
1 thyme sprig, or 1 teaspoon dried
Salt

Pour the browning sauce into a large, heavy casserole and set over medium heat. Add the meats and all the remaining ingredients. Add water to cover and bring to a boil. Skim, reduce the heat and simmer for 45 minutes. Allow to cool. Cover and refrigerate for 24 hours.

Remove the pepperpot from the refrigerator and bring to room temperature, about 1 hour.

Preheat the oven to 350° F.

Cover the casserole and bake for 1 hour, until heated through.

Serve in heated soup plates with boiled rice and beans.

Serves 6 to 8

Chicken with Coconut Curry Sauce

An abundance of dishes with curry and coconut are popular in the islands. Use the best-quality curry you can find.

3 cups fresh or canned chicken stock
½ cup freshly grated coconut
¼ cup vegetable oil
Salt and freshly ground pepper
8 chicken pieces (about 2 pounds)
All-purpose flour for dusting
1 large onion, chopped
1 tablespoon curry powder, or to taste
3 ripe tomatoes, peeled, seeded and chopped
1 green bell pepper, seeded and chopped
4 saffron threads, crumbled

In a small saucepan, combine the stock and coconut and bring to a boil over medium heat. Reduce the heat and simmer for 15 minutes. Set aside to cool for at least 15 minutes.

Meanwhile, in a large nonreactive sauté pan, heat the oil over medium heat. Salt and pepper the chicken pieces and dust with flour. Add the chicken to the pan and sauté on both sides until golden. Remove and set aside.

Pour off most of the oil from the pan, add the onion and sauté until wilted. Stir in the curry and cook for 1 to 2 minutes, or until the curry is absorbed. Add the tomatoes and bell pepper and cook for 1 to 2 minutes. Mix in the saffron and the chicken. Strain the stock over the chicken and bring to a boil. Reduce the heat and simmer for 10 minutes, until the chicken is heated through.

Serve with boiled white rice.

Serves 4

Sancocho
OXTAIL STEW

In a variation of this meat-based stew, Trinidad cooks will often include fresh coconut milk.

3 pounds oxtail, cut into 1½-inch pieces
Juice of 1 orange, preferably Seville
3 tablespoons red wine vinegar
Salt and freshly ground pepper
¼ cup olive oil
1 tablespoon raw cane sugar or light brown sugar
3 medium onions, chopped
3 celery ribs, chopped
3 medium carrots, chopped
4 garlic cloves, chopped
5 cups fresh or canned chicken stock
1 cup dry red wine
2 allspice berries, crushed
1 Scotch bonnet pepper or other fresh hot chili pepper, seeded, deveined and chopped
1 tablespoon chopped coriander
1 thyme sprig
1 bay leaf, crushed
1 strip orange zest (2 inches)
4 ripe tomatoes, peeled, seeded and chopped; or 2 cups canned plum tomatoes

In a large bowl, toss the meat with the orange juice, vinegar, and salt and pepper to taste. Cover and marinate for 1 hour.

In a large nonreactive heavy skillet, heat the oil over medium heat. Remove the meat from the bowl and reserve the juices. Sprinkle the meat with the sugar and brown the meat on all sides. Remove the meat and reserve.

Add the onions to the skillet and sauté over medium heat until translucent. Add the celery, carrots and garlic and sauté for 5 minutes. Add the meat juices, stock, wine, allspice, chili pepper, coriander, thyme, bay leaf and orange zest. Bring to a boil; reduce the heat to a simmer. Add the tomatoes and meat, cover and simmer for 1½ hours, or until the meat is fork-tender. (At this point the stew will be tastier if cooled and refrigerated and served hot the following day with fresh-cooked vegetables.)

Season to taste and serve with boiled white rice or any combination of boiled plantains, calabaza, cassava and Caribbean yams.

Serves 4 to 6

Turkey Stew

Turkeys were wild game for the Arawaks long before the colonists domesticated the birds—and turkey remains favorite fare in the islands today.

6 garlic cloves, minced
1 Scotch bonnet pepper or other fresh
    hot chili pepper, seeded, deveined
    and minced
1 teaspoon dried thyme
2 tablespoons chopped fresh
    parsley
1 bay leaf, crushed
¼ cup orange juice, preferably
    Seville
1 turkey breast (8 to 10 pounds), boned
    and skinned, the meat cubed
¼ cup olive oil
2 medium onions, chopped
1 medium red bell pepper, seeded and
    diced
1 cup Sofrito (page 137)
1 tablespoon tomato paste
2 cups fresh or canned turkey or chicken
    stock
1½ cups dry red wine
1½ pounds cassava or potatoes, peeled
    and cut into 1-inch cubes
½ cup dark rum
1 cup pitted green olives

In a large bowl, combine the garlic, chili pepper, thyme, parsley, bay leaf and orange juice. Add the turkey cubes, cover and refrigerate for 3 hours or overnight.

Remove the turkey from the refrigerator 30 minutes before cooking. Drain the meat and reserve the marinade.

In a heavy nonreactive skillet, heat enough of the oil to coat the bottom of the pan. Working in batches, lightly brown the turkey pieces, adding more oil as needed until all the pieces are browned. Set aside.

Add the remaining oil and onions to the skillet and sauté until translucent. Add the bell pepper and sauté an additional 5 minutes. Add the reserved marinade, Sofrito, tomato paste, stock and wine, and bring to a boil. Reduce the heat, cover and simmer for 1 hour, stirring from time to time.

Add the cassava cubes and cook for 20 minutes, or until tender.

In a small saucepan, warm the rum over medium heat. Carefully pour the rum into the stew, add the olives and simmer for 10 minutes.

Serve with white rice and beans.

Serves 8 to 10

Creole Rabbit Stew

Like most stews, this one is best eaten the day after cooking.

3 tablespoons vegetable oil
2 teaspoons dark brown sugar or West Indian browning sauce
1 large rabbit, cut into small serving pieces (about 4 pounds)
Salt and freshly ground pepper
About ¼ cup all-purpose flour
4 shallots, finely chopped
3 garlic cloves, finely chopped
2 medium carrots, scraped and chopped
2 tablespoons tomato paste
Grated zest of ½ orange
Juice of 1 orange, preferably Seville
1 teaspoon dried oregano
2 teaspoons dried thyme
1¼ cups fresh or canned chicken stock
2 tablespoons flour kneaded with 2 tablespoons unsalted butter
2 Scotch bonnet chili peppers, seeded and finely chopped
½ cup dark rum
1 tablespoon chopped fresh parsley

In a large, heavy sauté pan heat the oil with the brown sugar over medium heat. Allow to brown slightly but without burning; if it begins to smoke, lift from the heat for a few seconds. Sprinkle the rabbit pieces with salt and pepper and lightly dust with flour. Sauté until golden brown on all sides. Remove from the pan and reserve.

Stir the shallots, garlic, carrots, tomato paste, orange zest, orange juice, oregano, thyme and chicken stock into the pan. Bring to a boil. Crumble the kneaded flour and butter mixture into the liquid. Stir briskly until the flour mixture dissolves.

Add the chili peppers and rabbit pieces. Cover and simmer for 45 to 60 minutes, or until the rabbit is tender.

In a small saucepan, warm the rum. Carefully pour over the rabbit and simmer for 5 minutes. Taste for seasoning. Remove the rabbit to a serving platter. Cover with sauce and sprinkle with parsley. Serve with boiled white rice.

Serves 4

Pork & Pig's Tail Stew

Pig's tails add authenticity to this dish, delicious even without them.

3 tablespoons vegetable oil
2 pounds lean pork, cubed
1 medium onion, chopped
2 garlic cloves, chopped
4 scallions (including some of the green), chopped
1 small chili pepper, seeded and chopped
4 pickled pig's tails, cut into ½-inch pieces (optional)
1 tablespoon West Indian browning sauce, or substitute raw cane sugar
2 large tomatoes, peeled, seeded and chopped
1½ cups dried small white navy beans, soaked overnight
2 cups fresh or canned chicken stock
1 cup fresh Coconut Milk (page 139) or canned unsweetened
1 teaspoon minced fresh thyme, or ½ teaspoon dried
1 teaspoon minced fresh oregano, or ½ teaspoon dried

In a large nonreactive skillet, heat the oil over medium heat. Add the cubed pork and sauté until golden on all sides. Remove the meat from the pan and reserve. Add the onion, garlic and scallions, and sauté until the onion is translucent. Stir in the chili pepper, pig's tails, browning sauce and tomatoes. Bring to a simmer.

Fold in the beans, pork, stock, coconut milk, and water to cover. Bring to a simmer. Add the herbs and simmer for 1 hour, or until the beans are tender.

Serve with boiled white rice.

Serves 4 to 5

Squid & Red Bean Stew

This is a favorite fishermen's dish in the small villages of Martinique.

3 bacon slices
2 tablespoons olive oil
6 scallions (including some of the green), chopped
1 garlic clove, minced
1 celery rib, chopped
2 medium tomatoes, peeled, seeded and chopped
1 Scotch bonnet or other hot chili pepper, seeded and minced
1 teaspoon chopped fresh thyme, or ¼ teaspoon dried
2 cups cooked kidney beans
Pinch of ground cinnamon
Salt
1 pound squid, cleaned, mantle cut into ½-inch rings and tentacles chopped
Juice of 1 lime

In a nonreactive skillet, render the bacon until golden; drain and set aside.

Pour off most of the bacon fat and add the oil, scallions, garlic and celery; sauté over medium heat until they begin to sweat out their juices, about 3 minutes. Add the tomatoes, chili pepper and thyme; bring to a simmer. Cook for 5 minutes. Add the beans, cinnamon, and salt to taste, and cook for 10 minutes.

Chop the bacon and add to the mixture. Add the squid and cook for 5 minutes, or until the squid is just tender. Do not overcook or it will become rubbery.

Stir in the lime juice and serve at once.

Serves 4

Conch Stew

Nothing compares to the taste of fresh island conch, but the native Atlantic Coast variety offered stateside in Asian fish markets makes a reasonable substitute, as does canned conch.

¼ cup olive oil
1 large onion, finely chopped
2 garlic cloves, minced
1 celery rib, finely chopped
1 carrot, finely chopped
1 red bell pepper, seeded and finely chopped
1 pound conch, pounded and ground (see Note)
3 large tomatoes, peeled, seeded and chopped; or 2 cups canned plum tomatoes
1 teaspoon chopped fresh thyme, or ½ teaspoon dried
1 teaspoon chopped fresh oregano, or ½ teaspoon dried

1 whole Scotch bonnet pepper; or 1 small hot chili pepper
4 cups Light Fish Stock (page 107)
Salt and freshly ground pepper
Dry sherry

In a large nonreactive stockpot, heat the oil over medium heat. Add the onion, garlic, celery, carrot and bell pepper, and sauté until the vegetables begin to sweat out their juices.

Add the conch and cook for another 2 minutes. Add the tomatoes, herbs, whole chili pepper and stock, and bring to a boil. Reduce the heat, season with salt and pepper and simmer for 30 minutes.

Remove the chili pepper. Serve the stew in heated bowls with 1 tablespoon of sherry added to each bowl.

Serves 6 or more

Note: When fresh conch is available, it is important to beat the flesh with a meat mallet for 10 minutes. It also can be tenderized through a meat grinder.

daube de Poisson
FISH STEW

Traditional French daube is made of beef slowly braised in dry red wine. In the French-speaking islands, however, daube is almost always made with fish.

MARINADE
¼ cup fresh lime juice
1 fresh Scotch bonnet or other fresh hot chili pepper, crushed
3 garlic cloves, crushed
1 teaspoon chopped fresh thyme
Salt
3 pounds fresh mako shark or swordfish steaks, cubed
About 2 cups cold water

SAUCE MIXTURE
All-purpose flour
4 tablespoons olive oil
1 medium onion, finely chopped
1 garlic clove, finely chopped
4 scallions (including some of the green), chopped
2 medium tomatoes, peeled, seeded and chopped
1 bay leaf
1 teaspoon fresh thyme, or ½ teaspoon dried
1 teaspoon fresh oregano, or ½ teaspoon dried
Salt and freshly ground pepper

½ cup Light Fish Stock (page 107)
1 tablespoon capers, drained (optional)
¼ cup fresh lime juice
2 tablespoons chopped parsley

To make the marinade: In a large bowl, mix the lime juice with the chili pepper, garlic, thyme, and salt to taste. Add the fish and enough cold water to cover. Cover and refrigerate for 1 hour.

Drain the fish and discard the marinade. Dust the fish lightly with flour.

In a large nonreactive heavy skillet, heat half the oil over medium heat and sauté the fish until golden on all sides; reserve. Add the remaining 2 tablespoons oil, the onion, garlic and scallions, and sauté until they sweat out their juices, about 5 minutes. Add the tomatoes, bay leaf, thyme, oregano, and salt and pepper to taste. Bring to a simmer and cook for 5 minutes.

Add the fish cubes and stock. Cook for 10 minutes, or until the fish is heated through.

Add the capers and lime juice. Ladle the daube into warm soup plates and sprinkle with the parsley.

Serves 4 to 6

Marinated Tuna with Curried Tomato Stew

This marinade proved to be a successful holiday solution for leftover vegetables.

FISH AND MARINADE
¼ cup low-sodium soy sauce
2 tablespoons dark rum
1 tablespoon vegetable oil
1 tablespoon brown sugar
2 teaspoons Dijon mustard
1 teaspoon grated fresh ginger
1 pound fresh tuna steak, cut 1-inch thick

STEW
2 tablespoons olive oil
4 scallions (including some of the green), chopped
1 tablespoon curry powder
4 large ripe tomatoes, peeled, seeded and chopped; or 3 cups canned plum tomatoes
Salt and freshly ground pepper
¼ cup fresh passion fruit juice; or
    2 tablespoons fresh orange juice plus
    2 tablespoons fresh lime juice

To prepare the fish and marinade: Combine the soy sauce, rum, vegetable oil, sugar, mustard and ginger in a baking dish. Add the fish to the dish, and coat both sides with the marinade. Refrigerate for 1 hour.

To prepare the stew: Heat the olive oil in a large nonreactive saucepan over medium heat. Add the scallions and cook until limp. Add the curry powder and cook for 1 to 2 minutes. Add the tomatoes, and salt and pepper to taste. Simmer for 15 minutes. Stir in the fruit juice and set the pan aside.

Remove the fish from the marinade and pat dry with paper towels. Cube the fish and set aside.

Place a large nonstick skillet over high heat. When the skillet is very hot, add the fish cubes and sear quickly, shaking the pan. Add the curry-tomato mixture, reduce the heat and simmer until the stew is just heated through; the fish should be pink to rare.

Serve in warm soup plates, with boiled white rice.

Serves 4

Spain

from the beginning imported cattle, pigs, sheep, goats and horses to the islands. So swift was their success with livestock that within a decade of Columbus's discovery, Hispaniola and Jamaica were supplying their own meat, as well as provisioning the conquistadors who would eventually overwhelm all of South America.

The Arawaks cooked their wild boar and turtle on a precursor to our barbecue called a *barbacoa,* a grating of thin green sticks woven like a wire mattress and tied to posts like a raised bed. The meat was sliced in strips, laid on the *barbacoa* and cooked slowly, to permeate it with pungent wood smoke from the fire beneath.

Pan-Caribbean cuisine reflects an amalgam of the Old and New Worlds, and meat dishes are prime examples. Cuba's chopped or shredded beef *picadillo,* based on an old Moorish dish made with olives and raisins, also contains the tomatoes and hot peppers of the islands. *Ropa vieja,* which literally means "old clothes," is a traditional beef dish that migrated early on from Spain; the shredded beef is said to resemble old rags, hence its name. The Dominican Republic's *carne mechada*—a stuffing of ham, capers, garlic, peppers and onions for beef and pork—derived from the Spanish mainland. What makes it Caribbean is the use of native ingredients like annatto seed oil, hot peppers, spices, fruits and vegetables. The Cubans, for instance, add raisins, prunes, cheese and hard-cooked eggs.

Roasted pork is another native favorite, and every part of the pig can be an inspiration to the cook. Many Spanish-speaking islanders are partial to *chicharrones,* or fried pork cracklings. Jamaicans thrive on jerked pork—named for the highly spiced meld of seasonings used to marinate their meats before grilling. There are jerk pits—little huts and lean-tos that dot the highways and byways—all over the island, where Jamaicans gather to feast on their national dish.

Goats have the run of most islands—a common sight, surveying the local scene from atop abandoned rusting trucks, or in small herds scattering the crowds at beach picnics. Eventually they find their way to the local butcher, and then the cooking pot. Fragrant goat curries are Caribbean specialties, served with rice and fruit chutneys or stuffed into roti. When goat cannot be had, the second choice is lamb.

In the nineteenth century, everyone from plantation owners to peasants viewed meat as a sign of status and a gift of generous welcome to a guest. This custom endures.

Baked Fresh Ham Criolla

This Creole version of a baked fresh ham is served throughout the spring, beginning with the Easter celebrations.

1 small fresh ham (6 to 7 pounds)
12 large garlic cloves, peeled
2 tablespoons chopped fresh oregano
1 tablespoon chopped fresh thyme
1 tablespoon ground cumin
1 tablespoon dry mustard
1 small pimiento
1 Scotch bonnet or other fresh hot chili
    pepper, seeded
Coarse salt
Grated zest and juice (about ¾ cup) of
    1 bitter orange, preferably Seville, or
    substitute navel
3 cups fresh orange juice
4 medium onions, thinly sliced

Score the ham and set aside.

In a food processor, puree the garlic, oregano, thyme, cumin, dry mustard, pimiento, chili pepper, and salt to taste.

Add the zest and juice of the bitter orange and blend.

Spread the puree over the ham and cover and refrigerate for 12 hours or overnight.

Remove from the refrigerator 2 hours before cooking time. Wipe the ham dry with a paper towel.

Preheat the oven to 450° F.

Place the ham on a rack and set in a roasting pan. Pour the orange juice into the pan and cover the ham's surface with the onion slices. Reduce the heat to 325° and bake for 30 minutes per pound, basting frequently. The ham is done when the internal temperature registers 170° F., or when the juices run clear when pierced with a knife. Allow to cool for 15 minutes before slicing.

Serve with Mango Relish (page 136), rice and beans or assorted boiled root vegetables.

Serves 8 to 10

Griots

GLAZED PORK CUBES

Although this dish is a Haitian specialty, the cooking method is almost identical in the Spanish-speaking islands.

3 pounds pork shoulder with bone, cut into 2-inch cubes; or 2 pounds pork tenderloin, all fat removed, cut into 1-inch cubes
1 large onion, chopped
3 scallions (including some of the green), trimmed and sliced
1 thyme sprig, or ½ teaspoon dried
¾ cup fresh orange juice, preferably Seville
¼ cup fresh lime juice
1 fresh hot red or green chili pepper, seeded, deveined and finely diced
2 garlic cloves, finely chopped
Salt
1 cup all-purpose flour
¼ teaspoon ground cinammon
½ teaspoon ground cumin
½ cup peanut or vegetable oil, for frying

In a large nonreactive casserole, mix the pork cubes with the onion, scallions, thyme, orange juice, lime juice, chili pepper, garlic and salt to taste. Cover and refrigerate for 6 hours or overnight.

Add enough cold water to cover the meat. Cover the casserole and bring to a boil over high heat. Reduce the heat and simmer for 1 hour, or until the meat is fork-tender. Remove the meat and allow to cool thoroughly; discard the cooking liquid and solids.

In a mixing bowl, sift the flour with the cinnamon and cumin and lightly dust the pork cubes with the flour mixture.

Coat a large heavy skillet with half of the oil and place over high heat until the oil begins to smoke. Working in batches, add half the pork cubes and fry, turning often, until browned and crusty on all sides. Remove the meat and drain on paper towels. Add more oil as needed and repeat with the remaining pork.

Serve warm, with Sauce Ti-Malice (page 135).

Serves 6 to 8

Caribbean Meat Salad

Any leftover boiled or roasted meat or chicken will do just fine for this salad.

2 heads Bibb lettuce, washed and dried
About 2 pounds cold boiled or roasted
    beef, trimmed and cubed
2 cups fresh pineapple, cut into small
    cubes
2 oranges, preferably Seville, zest and
    membrane removed and cut into
    sections
1 lime, zest and membrane removed and
    cut into sections
2 tablespoons chopped fresh coriander
¼ cup extra-virgin olive oil
Salt and freshly ground pepper

Mound the lettuce on 4 large salad plates. Arrange the meat, pineapple, orange and lime sections and their juice on top. Sprinkle each plate with some of the coriander.

Sprinkle on the olive oil and season generously with salt and pepper.

Serves 4

Curried Goat or Lamb

Curried goat is served with white rice, and quite often is the filling for the rotis sold from carts and trucks at lunchtime.

4 pounds goat or lamb shoulder, trimmed,
    meat cubed
3 garlic cloves, minced
3 tablespoons curry powder
1 Scotch bonnet or other fresh hot chili
    pepper, seeded and finely chopped
Salt and pepper
¼ cup peanut oil
2 small onions, chopped
2 large tomatoes, peeled, seeded and
    chopped
4 cups fresh or canned chicken stock
1 tablespoon tomato paste
2 teaspoons chopped fresh coriander

Place the meat in a large bowl and add the garlic, curry powder, chili pepper, and salt and pepper to taste. Mix well and set aside to marinate for 1 hour.

Heat the oil in a large nonreactive skillet until very hot. Add the meat and brown on all sides. Remove the meat and set aside.

Reduce the heat under the skillet and add the onions. Cook until wilted. Add the meat, tomatoes, stock and tomato paste. Cover and cook over low heat for 3 hours, or until the meat is tender. Add more stock or water, if necessary. The meat should be falling apart.

Stir in the coriander and taste for seasoning. Serve over white rice or with warm roti.

Serves 4 to 6

Cuban Pot Roast

Simple roasts and meats are turned into spicy, flavorful dishes with the addition of *sofrito,* the mother of most Cuban stews and meat.

¼ cup all-purpose flour
1 teaspoon ground cumin
Salt and freshly ground pepper
4 ounces smoked bacon, thickly sliced
    and cut into ¼-inch cubes
1 eye of round beef roast, trimmed and
    tied (about 5 pounds)
3 tablespoons olive oil
2 large onions, thinly sliced
3 garlic cloves, chopped
1 celery rib, chopped
1 medium carrot, chopped
2 cups fresh or canned beef or chicken
    stock
½ cup dry red wine
1½ cups Sofrito (page 137)
1 rosemary sprig
1 thyme sprig
1 bay leaf
3 strips orange zest
12 prunes, pitted (optional)

In a shallow pan, mix the flour, cumin, and salt and pepper to taste. Set aside.

In a heavy casserole, render the bacon over medium heat until golden. Remove the bacon with a slotted spoon and drain on paper towels. Keep the casserole over medium heat.

Dust the roast in the flour mixture. Place it in the bacon fat; brown on all sides until golden and crusty. Set aside.

Reduce the heat and add the oil, onions, garlic, celery and carrot to the casserole. Sauté the vegetables until they begin to sweat out their juices, about 10 minutes. Add the stock, wine, Sofrito, herbs, bay leaf and zest, and bring to a boil. Return the roast to the casserole and reduce the heat to a simmer; cover and cook for 2 hours.

Remove the herb sprigs, bay leaf and zest. Add prunes and bacon; simmer for 30 minutes, until the roast is fork-tender.

Serve with boiled root vegetables and a garlic puree.

Serves 6

Jerked Pork

The term *jerk* is both a reference to the seasonings used in preparing the meat before cooking and to the way each portion is chopped or shredded.

6 pounds pork shoulder or ribs

MARINADE
8 scallions (including some of the green), finely chopped
1 medium onion, finely chopped
4 garlic cloves, minced
2 to 3 Scotch bonnet or other fresh hot chili peppers, seeded, deveined and finely chopped
2 teaspoons minced fresh thyme, or 1 teaspoon dried
About 1 teaspoon salt
1 teaspoon raw cane sugar or light brown sugar
1 teaspoon ground allspice
½ teaspoon ground nutmeg
½ teaspoon ground cinnamon
1 teaspoon freshly ground black pepper

2 teaspoons cider vinegar
¼ cup vegetable oil

Combine all the marinade ingredients in a large bowl. Place the pork in a roasting pan and coat with the marinade. Cover and refrigerate for at least 4 hours or overnight.

Prepare a charcoal grill. When the coals glow dusty red, push the coals to the sides and place a foil drip pan in the center; arrange the coals around the pan to provide indirect heat. Place the pork in the center of the grill over the drip pan. Turn and brush the meat with the marinade as often as possible for about 1½ hours. Add more coals if the heat begins to flag.

Remove the pork to a chopping board. Chop with a cleaver into 1-inch pieces.

Serve with Pickapeppa Sauce and grill-roasted sweet potatoes or yams.

Serves 4 to 6

Note: This marinade is enough to grill 3 split chickens, 6 pounds of large shrimp or prawns in their shells, a dozen blue-claw crabs or 18 rock lobster tails.

Jug-jug

Jug-jug is a dish Baijans dote on. The Barbados version of *haggis*, it is served in Scots tradition on New Year's Day.

½ **pound trimmed lean corned beef**
½ **pound chuck beef or lean pork loin**
1 whole Scotch bonnet pepper or small hot chili pepper
1 medium onion, halved
2 celery ribs, chopped
2 garlic cloves, crushed
2 whole cloves
1 tablespoon dried thyme
1 pound fresh or canned green pigeon peas (*gandules*)
¼ **cup corn flour**
2 tablespoons unsalted butter
Salt and freshly ground pepper

In a medium nonreactive soup pot, add the corned beef and chuck beef, chili pepper, onion, celery, garlic, cloves and thyme. Cover with cold water and bring to a boil over high heat. Reduce the heat and simmer for 1 hour, or until the meat is fork-tender.

Strain and reserve the stock. Remove the meat from the vegetables and reserve. Discard the vegetables.

Return the stock to the pot and add the peas and enough water to cover. Bring to a boil, reduce the heat and simmer for 20 minutes, or until the peas are tender. (If using canned peas, add to the stock and heat through.) Strain the peas and reserve the stock.

In a food processor, puree the meat and peas until smooth. Set aside.

In a medium saucepan, heat 2 cups of reserved stock, or add enough water to make 2 cups. Over medium heat, bring the stock to a boil and add the corn flour in a steady stream. Stir constantly with a wooden spoon. When the mixture begins to thicken, add the meat and pea mixture. Cook over low heat for 15 minutes, stirring constantly, or until the mixture is thick. Fold in the butter and season with salt and pepper to taste. Place the mixture in a small crock. Jug-jug will keep for days in the refrigerator.

Serve warm with holiday ham.

Serves 6 or more

Tender Tenderloin

Marinating this cut or lesser cuts of beef in papaya juice, a natural tenderizer, will make the meat more buttery.

1 pound beef tenderloin, cut into 4 slices, each about 4 ounces
1 medium papaya, peeled, seeded and chopped
Juice of 1 lime
Salt and freshly ground pepper
2 tablespoons vegetable oil
2 tablespoons unsalted butter
¼ cup heavy cream

Place the slices of tenderloin in a small glass baking dish. Mix the papaya and lime juice and pour over the meat. Cover and refrigerate for 2 hours, turning a couple of times.

When ready to cook, remove the beef from the marinade and pat dry with paper towels. Reserve the marinade. Season the meat with salt and pepper to taste.

Heat the oil and butter in a nonreactive skillet over high heat. Sear the meat on both sides to the desired state of doneness. Remove and keep warm.

Pour off most of the fat in the skillet. Add the cream and bring to a boil. Cook until reduced by about one-third. Stir in the reserved marinade; season with salt to taste.

Place 1 slice of tenderloin on each of 4 dinner plates. Spoon some of the sauce over each portion.

Serves 4

Bistec a la Criolla

Bistec is a delicious and gutsy beef dish almost always paired with boiled roots —cassava, yams, turnips and carrots. A bowl of boiled and pureed garlic laced with olive oil often accompanies these vegetables.

1 medium onion, finely chopped
2 garlic cloves, minced
¼ cup chopped fresh parsley
Juice of 1 bitter orange, preferably Seville; or juice of ½ lemon plus ½ orange or 1 lemon
Salt and freshly ground pepper
6 slices beef top or bottom round steaks, cut ¼ inch thick and pounded flat
About ⅓ cup olive oil
4 tablespoons unsalted butter

In a bowl, combine the onion, garlic, parsley, orange or lemon juice, and salt and pepper to taste. Spread a little of the mixture over each side of the steaks. Cover for 1 hour.

In a large, heavy skillet that will comfortably hold 2 to 3 of the steaks, heat enough of the oil to coat the pan. Scrape the seasoning mixture off the steaks and reserve it.

When the oil begins to smoke, brown the steaks over high heat for 2 to 4 minutes on each side, depending on the degree of doneness desired. Remove to a warm serving platter and continue to cook the remaining steaks.

Add the reserved seasoning mixture and juices to the pan and quickly stir in the butter until it melts completely.

Pour over the steaks and serve.

Serves 6

graziella's Picadillo
BEEF HASH

I have a special fondness for this highly seasoned hash. It is a favorite Saturday-night supper served by Cuban friends—and when I am invited to their home, it is the treat of my weekend.

½ cup dark raisins
½ cup dark rum
1 tablespoon annatto oil
2 tablespoons olive oil
1 large onion, finely chopped
1 large green bell pepper, seeded and finely chopped
2 garlic cloves, minced
1 small hot chili pepper, seeded, deveined and chopped
2 pounds ground chuck
8 ounces ground lean pork
2 large tomatoes, peeled, seeded and chopped; or 2 cups canned plum tomatoes
½ teaspoon ground cumin
Salt and freshly ground pepper
¼ cup pimiento-stuffed green olives, chopped
1 tablespoon capers, drained
1 bay leaf, crushed
1 cup fresh or canned beef or chicken stock

Place the raisins in a small bowl and cover with the rum. Set aside.

In a large nonreactive heavy skillet, heat the annatto oil and olive oil over medium heat. Add the onion, bell pepper, garlic and chili pepper, and cook until the onion is wilted, about 8 minutes.

Add the meats and cook, stirring, until lightly browned all over. Add the tomatoes, cumin, and salt and pepper to taste. Simmer, stirring from time to time, for 15 minutes.

Add the raisins and rum, chopped green olives, capers, bay leaf and stock, and simmer for 45 minutes, stirring from time to time.

Serve with plain, boiled white rice, black beans and fried ripe plantains or plantain chips.

Serves 6

Pork in Tamarind Sauce

Tamarind, thick as apple butter, is also an important ingredient in Worcestershire sauce.

2½ pounds lean boneless pork, cut into
    1½-inch cubes
2 tablespoons low-sodium soy sauce
3 garlic cloves, minced
1 medium onion, chopped
1 teaspoon fresh thyme, or ½ teaspoon
    dried
1 teaspoon fresh oregano, or ½ teaspoon
    dried
Salt and freshly ground pepper
¼ cup vegetable oil
2 cups fresh or canned chicken stock
3 tablespoons tamarind sauce
1 tablespoon dry sherry
1 celery rib, chopped
1 teaspoon cornstarch
1 tablespoon cold water

In a large bowl, mix the cubed meat with the soy sauce, garlic, chopped onion, thyme, oregano, and salt and freshly ground pepper to taste. Cover and allow to marinate for 1 hour.

In a large skillet, heat the oil until almost smoking. Add the meat and brown over high heat. Drain off most of the oil and add the stock, tamarind sauce, sherry and celery. Reduce the heat and simmer for 1¼ hours, stirring occasionally, or until the meat is fork-tender and the liquid reduces to about one-third.

Dissolve the cornstarch in the cold water. Add to the mixture and stir until the sauce thickens and becomes shiny. Remove from the heat.

Serve with boiled white rice and Dhal (page 113).

Serves 4

Ropa Vieja
OLD CLOTHES

Boiling and then braising meats is a tenderizing trick for second cuts.

3 pounds boneless flank steak or skirt
    steak
1 carrot, peeled and roughly chopped
1 celery rib, roughly chopped
1 large onion, cut in half
1 bay leaf
6 peppercorns
3 tablespoons olive oil
1 medium Spanish onion, thinly sliced
2 garlic cloves, finely chopped
1 medium green bell pepper, seeded and
    cut in thin strips
1 medium red bell pepper, seeded and cut
    in thin strips
1 small fresh hot red or green chili
    pepper, seeded, deveined and
    chopped
1 large tomato, peeled and chopped; or
    1 cup canned plum tomatoes
1 teaspoon fresh thyme, or ½ teaspoon
    dried
1 teaspoon fresh oregano, or ½ teaspoon
    dried
⅛ teaspoon ground allspice
¼ cup dry red wine
Salt and freshly ground pepper

Place the steak in a large nonreactive casserole and add the carrot, celery, onion, bay leaf and peppercorns. Add enough cold water to cover and bring to a boil over high heat. Reduce the heat and simmer for 1½ hours, or until the steak is tender. Remove the steak from the liquid to cool; strain the liquid and reserve. When cool enough to handle, shred or cut the steak into fine strips.

In a large heavy skillet, heat the oil over medium heat. Add the Spanish onion slices, garlic, green and red bell peppers and chili pepper, and sauté until the onion and peppers are tender, about 8 minutes. Add the tomato, thyme, oregano, allspice, wine, 1 cup of the reserved cooking liquid, and salt and pepper to taste. Bring to a simmer and cook for 5 minutes.

Add the shredded steak and cook for 15 minutes, stirring from time to time. Add more cooking liquid if necessary; the dish should be moist, with enough sauce to accompany the rice.

Serve over boiled white rice and black beans.

Serves 6

Smothered Rabbit

The cooking methods of Spain prevail throughout Puerto Rico and Cuba. Olive is almost always the oil of choice; butter is rarely used.

2½ pounds rabbit, cut into serving pieces
10 garlic cloves, thinly sliced
1 cup dry sherry or amber rum
2 teaspoons minced fresh oregano, or
    1 teaspoon dried
⅛ teaspoon cayenne pepper
Salt and freshly ground pepper
¼ cup olive oil
1 medium onion, chopped
2 ripe tomatoes, peeled, seeded and
    chopped; or 1 cup canned plum
    tomatoes
1 medium green bell pepper, seeded,
    deveined and chopped
1 medium red bell pepper, seeded,
    deveined and chopped
½ Scotch bonnet or other fresh hot chili
    pepper, seeded, deveined and finely
    chopped
2 cups fresh or canned chicken stock
½ cup dry white wine
2 ripe plantains, peeled and sliced into 1-
    inch rounds
2 tablespoons capers, drained

In a large bowl, mix the rabbit pieces with the garlic, sherry, oregano, cayenne, and salt and pepper to taste. Cover and refrigerate for 2 hours.

In a large, heavy casserole, heat the oil over medium heat. Add the onion and sauté until translucent. Add the tomatoes, green and red bell peppers and chili pepper, and simmer for 10 minutes. Add the rabbit, marinade, stock and wine, and bring to a boil. Skim and reduce the heat to a simmer. Cover and cook for 1½ hours. Add the plantains and cook for an additional 15 minutes. Add the capers and continue cooking until the rabbit is fork-tender.

Serve in heated bowls with boiled white rice and black or kidney beans.

Serves 6

Roast Leg of Lamb, Creole Style

The subtle flavor of fresh oregano is a nice change from tried-and-true mint.

1 small leg of lamb (about 5 pounds)
3 garlic cloves, slivered
Olive oil
½ cup finely chopped fresh oregano
Salt and freshly ground pepper
¼ cup dark rum
1½ cups lamb or chicken stock
1 tablespoon Worcestershire sauce

With a paring knife, score the meaty surface of the lamb and insert the garlic slivers into the meat.

Place the lamb in a large nonreactive pan and coat it with olive oil. Spread the surface with the oregano and coat liberally with salt and pepper. Cover and refrigerate overnight.

Remove the lamb from the refrigerator 1 hour before roasting.

Preheat the oven to 450° F.

Place the lamb on a rack in a roasting pan and reduce the heat to 350° F. Roast for 1¾ hours for medium-rare to rare. Transfer the roast to a warm platter and allow to rest for 15 minutes while you make the sauce.

Spoon off the fat and place the roasting pan over medium heat. Add the rum and stock and deglaze the pan, scraping up the brown bits. Bring to a boil and cook for 5 minutes, or until the sauce begins to thicken. Add the Worcestershire sauce and strain into a warm sauceboat.

Serve with guava jelly and boiled root vegetables.

Serves 6 to 8

froM

island to island the sound is the same—the country clatter of one or two chickens, three at most, pecking and meandering about.

The crow of the cock wakes you in the little cities, the country inn or the back side of the ocean-view hotel when you haven't been lucky enough to secure a room close to the sand. The humblest shack, the sugar-colored Victorian gingerbread house, the white-washed volcanic rock mansion—all have their resident chicken. The cock may be raised to become a fighter, but usually the plume-footed bantam or the speckled hen is there for the eggs or the pot.

The backyard chicken goes back to the days when there was neither refrigeration nor supermarkets. Both are to be found in most contemporary Caribbean towns and cities, but tradition can be stronger than progress. Chickens, as indigenous to the islands as coconuts, are likely to be part of the family menagerie—in some cases replacing a watch dog. Local townsfolk still buy chickens live at the daily outdoor markets.

The versatility of the chicken is remarkable in any cuisine, but Caribbean recipes for chicken are especially brilliant and varied. *Chicharrones de pollo*—small fried pieces of chicken resembling their pork counterpart—are less greasy and messy than our fried chicken, and a *poulet colombo* sweating in curry or bathed in coconut milk or stewed in ginger and lime can rival any *coq au vin*.

A Haitian *poulet roti* stuffed with bread crumbs, bananas and spices or a chicken Creole marinated in citrus juices and served with green mangos is, by any standard, haute cuisine. Cooks in the Spanish islands create their own extraordinary version of traditional paella in *arroz con pollo*. And—although most island visitors will discover the culinary delights of duck with prunes or pineapple in Martinique, stuffed turkey in Puerto Rico, stewed turkey in Cuba, the sun-dried turkey from Haiti called *tassot dinde*, or turkey split and barbecued like Jamaican jerk—chicken remains the quintessential fowl of Caribbean choice.

Chicharrones de Pollo

These crisp and savory chicken morsels have only one thing in common with junk-food packets of fried pork skins— the name.

2 tablespoons dried oregano
1 tablespoon coarse salt
1 teaspoon freshly ground black pepper
½ cup fresh lime juice
4 pounds chicken, cut in 2-inch pieces,
    with the bone
All-purpose flour
About 1 cup peanut oil

In a large bowl, mix the oregano, salt, pepper and lime juice. Coat the chicken pieces with the mixture and add the lime juice. Cover and refrigerate for 4 hours or overnight, turning once or twice.

Remove the chicken pieces from the marinade and pat dry with paper towels. Dust lightly with flour.

In a large heavy skillet, heat half the oil over high heat. When the oil begins to shimmer, brown the chicken pieces, a few at a time, on all sides until crisp. Reserve the chicken in a warm oven. Add the remaining oil to the skillet and cook the remaining pieces.

Serve with boiled white rice, beans and plantain chips

Serves 6

Chicken Marinated with Grapefruit

The Caribbean is strong on citrus. This recipe is from a Cuban friend living in Miami, who says, "I used to use bitter oranges, but now I've got a grapefruit tree in the backyard."

3 pounds skinned and boned chicken
    pieces
1 cup fresh grapefruit juice
Juice of 1 lime
1 garlic clove, minced
1 tablespoon freshly grated ginger
1 teaspoon chopped fresh thyme, or
    ½ teaspoon dried
1 tablespoon molasses
1 tablespoon brown sugar

Wash the chicken pieces and pat dry with paper towels. Place the chicken in a baking dish and set aside.

In a bowl, combine the remaining ingredients and blend well. Pour the mixture over the chicken. Cover and refrigerate for 6 hours, or overnight, turning once or twice

Preheat the oven to 350° F.

Remove the chicken from the refrigerator. Drain off the marinade and reserve.

Bake the chicken, basting with some of the marinade from time to time, for 1¼ hours, or until fork-tender.

Serve with boiled rice and beans.

Serves 4 to 6

Note: The marinade works well for charcoal-grilled chicken as well.

Chicken in Almond Sauce

Mainland imports like olive oil, olives, saffron and almonds have been staples in the Spanish islands since sometime in the sixteenth century.

4 pounds chicken, cut into serving pieces
All-purpose flour, for dusting
4 tablespoons olive oil
2 medium onions, finely chopped
2 garlic cloves, chopped
2 medium tomatoes, peeled, seeded and
    chopped; or 1 cup canned plum
    tomatoes
1 tablespoon chopped fresh Italian
    parsley
¼ teaspoon ground cinnamon
Pinch of ground cloves
½ cup blanched almonds
2 cups fresh or canned chicken stock
4 to 5 saffron threads, crumbled
Salt and freshly ground white pepper
2 teaspoons lime or lemon juice

Lightly dust the chicken pieces with flour.

In a heavy nonreactive skillet, heat half the oil over medium heat. Add the chicken and sauté until golden on all sides. Reserve.

Drain the oil from the skillet and add the remaining 2 tablespoons oil. Add the onions and garlic to the skillet and sauté until wilted. Add the tomatoes, parsley, cinnamon and cloves; simmer for 10 minutes.

In a food processor, pulverize the almonds until almost dust. Add the almonds, stock, saffron, and salt and pepper to taste to the skillet and bring to a boil.

Add the chicken; cover and simmer for 45 minutes, or until the chicken is fork-tender. Remove the chicken pieces to a serving platter and place in a warm oven. Skim off any fat from the sauce and boil until reduced to about 2 cups. Add the lime juice.

Remove the chicken from the oven and pour the sauce over the top. Serve with boiled white rice.

Serves 4

Chicken & Pigeon Peas

Some Caribbean cooks will stir a smidgeon of curry powder into this pot.

2 teaspoons distilled white vinegar
3 garlic cloves, minced
1 medium onion, chopped
1 tablespoon chopped celery
2 tablespoons chopped fresh chives
1 teaspoon chopped fresh thyme, or
   ½ teaspoon dried
1 teaspoon chopped fresh oregano, or
   ½ teaspoon dried
¼ cup amber rum
Salt and freshly ground pepper
4 pounds chicken, cut into 8 serving
   pieces
1 pound dried pigeon peas *(gandules)*,
   soaked
¼ cup vegetable oil
2 teaspoons raw cane sugar or light
   brown sugar
Fresh or canned chicken stock or
   water
1 tablespoon tomato paste
1 tablespoon chopped fresh parsley

In a small bowl, combine the vinegar, garlic, onion, celery, chives, thyme, oregano, rum, and salt and pepper to taste. Mix well and rub into the chicken pieces. Refrigerate for 1 hour.

Meanwhile, boil the peas in lightly salted water for 30 minutes, or until almost tender. Drain and set aside.

In a large skillet, heat the oil over medium-high heat. Add the sugar and when the oil begins to brown, add the chicken pieces and brown on all sides. When the moisture has evaporated, add any leftover seasoning mixture and the peas. Add enough stock or water to cover and simmer for 35 to 40 minutes, or until the chicken is fork-tender. Remove the chicken to a heated serving platter.

Whisk the tomato paste into the pea mixture and cook for 3 minutes.

Pour the sauce over the chicken and sprinkle with the parsley.

Serves 4

Roast Chicken, Creole Style

This recipe is a delicious example of Haitian ingenuity when it comes to preparing stuffed chicken.

8 tablespoons (1 stick) unsalted butter, softened
1 garlic clove, minced
2 tablespoons fresh bread crumbs
Juice and grated zest of 1 lime
3 tablespoons plus 1 teaspoon dark rum
1 teaspoon raw cane sugar or light brown sugar
¼ teaspoon ground nutmeg
¼ teaspoon cayenne pepper
Salt and freshly ground pepper
3 ripe bananas
1 roasting chicken
1 cup fresh or canned chicken stock

Preheat the oven to 350° F.

In a large skillet, melt 4 tablespoons of the butter over medium heat. Add the garlic and bread crumbs and stir until crisp and lightly browned. Remove the skillet from the heat and stir in half the lime juice, 1 tablespoon of the rum, the sugar, nutmeg, cayenne, and salt and pepper to taste. Reserve.

In a medium bowl, mash the bananas with the remaining lime juice, the lime zest and 1 teaspoon of the rum. Fold in the bread crumbs and fill the cavity of the chicken with the mixture. Truss the chicken and rub the skin with the remaining 4 tablespoons butter. Place the chicken on a rack and set in a roasting pan. Roast for 1½ hours, or until the juices run clear.

Remove the bird from the pan and reserve on a warm platter. Spoon off most of the fat and place the roasting pan over high heat. Add the stock and bring to a boil, scraping the pan to release the browned bits.

Strain the sauce into a small saucepan. Set over medium heat, add the remaining 2 tablespoons of rum and carefully ignite. Shake the pan until the flames subside.

Serve the sauce with the chicken.

Serves 4

Chicken Oriental

The Chinese have had a great impact on the quality of produce grown and sold in Caribbean markets, and they have contributed many recipes to the island's culinary repertoire.

1 pound boneless chicken breast (about 2 breasts), cut diagonally into 1-inch-wide strips
1 small fresh hot chili pepper, seeded and cut into julienne
3 large garlic cloves, minced
Salt and freshly ground pepper
½ cup peanut oil
1 tablespoon sugar
1 piece of ginger with the skin (about 3 inches), thinly sliced
1 medium onion, sliced
1 red bell pepper, seeded and cut into strips
3 celery ribs, sliced
8 ounces fresh mushrooms, sliced
½ cup low-sodium soy sauce
¼ cup cornstarch
2 cups fresh or canned chicken stock

In a medium bowl, sprinkle the chicken pieces with the chili pepper, garlic, and salt and freshly ground pepper to taste. Set aside.

Heat ¼ cup of the oil in a hot wok. When very hot, fry the ginger until crisp and golden. Stir in the sugar. Add the chicken with the chili and garlic, and sauté until golden.

Remove the ginger and the chicken with a slotted spoon and set aside. Reduce the heat and sauté the vegetables, one at a time, and then add them to the reserved chicken.

In another medium bowl, stir the soy sauce and cornstarch into the stock. Add the mixture to the wok and simmer over low heat, stirring constantly, until the sauce is translucent. Add the chicken pieces and the vegetables to the sauce and heat through.

Serve immediately, with boiled white rice.

Serves 4 to 5

Poulet à la Creole

This spicy aromatic dish is one of the delights of the French islands from Haiti to Guadeloupe.

¼ cup peanut oil
4 pounds chicken, cut into serving pieces
3 large onions, thinly sliced
2 garlic cloves, chopped
1 tablespoon curry powder
5 saffron threads, crumbled
1 Scotch bonnet or other fresh hot chili pepper, seeded, deveined and minced
1 cup fresh Coconut Milk (page 139) or canned unsweetened
1 cup fresh or canned chicken stock
Salt and freshly ground pepper

In a large, deep skillet, heat the oil over medium heat. When the oil begins to shimmer, sauté the chicken pieces until golden on all sides. Reserve.

Pour off most of the fat, add the onions and garlic to the skillet and sauté until wilted. Stir in the curry powder, saffron and chili pepper, and cook for 3 or 4 minutes. Add the coconut milk, stock, and salt and pepper to taste.

Add the chicken to the skillet and bring to a simmer. Cover and cook for 45 minutes, or until the chicken is fork-tender. Serve with boiled white rice.

Serves 4

Violetta's Fried Chicken

These chicken morsels have a big bite!

8 pieces cut-up chicken (about 3 pounds)
Salt
1 medium onion, chopped
1 garlic clove, minced
1 teaspoon dried thyme
¼ teaspoon ground cumin
1 Scotch bonnet or other hot chili pepper, seeded and diced
Juice of 1 lime
¼ cup Pickapeppa Sauce

Wash the chicken pieces and pat dry with paper towels. Season with salt and place in a nonreactive baking dish.

In a small bowl, combine the onion, garlic, thyme, cumin, chili pepper, lime juice and Pickapeppa Sauce. Pour the sauce over the chicken and turn to coat each piece. Cover and refrigerate overnight.

Preheat the oven to 350° F.

Remove the chicken from the refrigerator and allow to stand for 30 minutes. Bake for about 1¼ hours, or until the chicken is fork-tender.

Serve with beans and rice.

Serves 4 to 6

Grilled Marinated Chicken Creole with Grilled Mangos & Bananas

Combining grilled chicken or meats with grilled fresh fruits is a time-honored practice of Haitian cooks. Marinating the chicken with three kinds of citrus juices adds a subtle piquance to the dish.

7 pounds cut-up chicken, for grilling
½ cup fresh orange juice
¼ cup fresh lime juice
¼ cup fresh lemon juice
½ cup dark rum
1 garlic clove, chopped
2 tablespoons raw cane sugar or light brown sugar
1 medium red or green bell pepper, seeded, deveined and chopped
1 medium sweet red onion, thinly sliced
3 tablespoons cider vinegar
2 tablespoons olive oil
Salt and freshly ground pepper
2 large mangos
Juice of 1 lime
3 ripe bananas
Vegetable oil, for the grill
2 tablespoons unsalted butter, melted

Cut away the chicken wings and reserve for another use. Wash and dry the chicken pieces. Arrange them in a single layer in a large baking dish.

In a medium bowl, combine the citrus juices, rum, garlic, sugar, bell pepper, onion, vinegar, olive oil, and salt and pepper to taste. Pour over the chicken pieces. Cover and refrigerate for 2 hours or overnight; turn the chicken once.

Prepare a charcoal fire 45 minutes before cooking time. Remove the chicken from the refrigerator 30 minutes before cooking time.

Peel and pit the mangos and cut into long 1-inch-wide slices. Place the slices on a sheet of foil, brush with lime juice and set aside. Peel the bananas, halve them lengthwise and brush with the lime juice. Place on the foil and set aside.

When the coals are ash-covered and glowing, lightly brush the grill with vegetable oil. Season the chicken with salt and pepper. Place the chicken pieces, cavity sides down, on the grill and cook for 10 minutes.

Turn and baste the chicken with the marinade and continue to cook for another 10 minutes. Baste and turn the chicken every 5 minutes for an additional 15 to 20 minutes, or until fork-tender.

Lightly brush the fruits with the melted butter. Set the foil on the grill during the last 10 minutes of cooking time. Perforate the foil to allow the heat to penetrate to the fruit. Fold the foil into packets, and cook until the fruits give off their juices, become slightly limp and are lightly charred.

Arrange the chicken on a heated platter and fan out the fruit at one end. Serve immediately.

Serves 6

Chicken Colombo

While Indian curry powder can be used for all Caribbean recipes, in French-speaking islands most cooks prepare their own versions.

3 tablespoons vegetable oil
4 pounds chicken, cut into serving pieces
1 medium onion, thinly sliced
2 garlic cloves, finely chopped
1 tablespoon curry powder (Colombo, page 138), or more to taste
Seeds from 2 cardamom pods
¾ cup fresh or canned chicken stock
¾ cup fresh or canned unsweetened coconut milk
1 tablespoon tomato paste
8 ounces calabaza (West Indian pumpkin), peeled and cubed
8 ounces christophine (chayote), peeled and cubed
8 ounces white Caribbean yam or potatoes, peeled and cubed
Salt and freshly ground pepper
Juice of 1 lime

In a large nonreactive heavy skillet, heat the oil over medium heat. Add the chicken pieces and sauté until golden on all sides. Remove the chicken and reserve.

Drain half the fat from the skillet and add the onion, garlic, curry and cardamom. Sauté for 8 minutes, or until the onion is translucent. Add the chicken stock, coconut milk and tomato paste, and simmer for 3 minutes. Add the chicken pieces, calabaza, christophine, Caribbean yam, and salt and pepper to taste. Cover the skillet and simmer for 40 minutes, or until the vegetables are tender.

When ready to serve, add the lime juice.

Serve with boiled white rice and Mango Relish (page 136).

Serves 4

Years

ago, on the Seven Mile Beach at Negril in Jamaica, before there were luxury hotels, I spent some time at a little inn, mostly walking along that sun-bleached stretch of sand. My encounters were few, except for several seven-year-olds who roamed the beach blowing tunes out of bright conch shells as pink as the soles of their feet. It was they who provided the daily catch of snapper, conch or spiny lobsters prepared by my innkeeper's cook—meals that far surpassed anything I might have been offered in the pleasure villas of Montego Bay.

For the visitor in the Caribbean, finding fresh fish is a game of chance. I always try the morning markets set up on the harbor docks of the larger towns, where farmers' wives, who have brought their fruits and vegetables, join the fishermen bargaining with the townsfolk and restaurateurs from their jostling boats—one skiff filled with conch, another with sea urchins, yet another with a rainbow array of local fish.

The Creoles of Martinique and Guadeloupe give us *blaff*, which begins with a simple broth—seasoned with allspice, cloves, scallions, fiery bonnet peppers, parsley, crushed garlic, lime juice and bay leaves—brought to a boil and slowly simmered. Then, as though slapping its way into the sea, the freshest fish go whole into the pot, are poached ever so briefly and are placed in each guest's bowl with a squeeze of lime.

Escabeche, the most popular fish dish in Puerto Rico and the Dominican Republic, is done the traditional Spanish way: olive oil, vinegar, onions and bay and allspice leaves are mixed with spices and poured over grilled or fresh filleted fish. For their *escovitch,* Jamaicans slit the fish, fill the pocket with fresh pepper and salt, then sear it in hot coconut oil. The marinade comes last.

Sopito is popular in the African-Dutch isles of Aruba and Curaçao, where almost every sort of fish is flavored with coconut milk and lime juice. Cubans sauté lobster meat in butter, simmer it in cream and eggs and finish it off with rum. It makes a truly glorified bisque served over a pile of fluffy rice.

Conch, or *lambi*—a mainstay almost everywhere in the islands—is served raw like seviche or in salads with oil, lemon and scallions. The people of Martinique and Guadeloupe make wonderful conch stews and chowders primed in brown sauce and flavored with nutmeg, cinnamon, thyme, hot chili peppers and lime juice—and sometimes served in pie shells or as little tarts.

The myth that Islanders favor meat over fish is false. The fact is that they are likely to eat more fish, and eat it fresher than we do, straight from the sea. It is the tourist who is apt to be dining on frozen shrimp and fillet of sole, flown rock-hard from the mainland to the major island airports.

Kingfish Cooked in Coconut Milk

More and more, kingfish is appearing on stateside menus and at our local fish-mongers. The combination of coconut milk and the acidic lime marinade intensifies the flavor of the fish.

MARINADE

4 kingfish fillets (about 8 ounces each), or substitute snapper, black bass or striped bass
½ cup fresh lime juice
1 fresh hot chili pepper, pounded
3 garlic cloves, minced
Salt
2 cups cold water

PREPARATION

3 tablespoons olive oil
6 shallots, minced
4 scallions (including some of the green), finely chopped
1 tablespoon chopped chives
2 teaspoons minced garlic
3 medium tomatoes, peeled, seeded and chopped
1 fresh hot green or red chili pepper, seeded and minced
3 tablespoons chopped fresh parsley
1 bay leaf, crushed
1 thyme sprig, or 2 teaspoons dried
Salt and freshly ground pepper
1 cup fresh Coconut Milk (page 139) or canned unsweetened
2 limes, halved

To marinate the fish: Arrange the fish fillets in a large, deep dish and sprinkle with the lime juice, chili pepper, minced garlic and salt to taste. Pour the cold water over the fish, cover and refrigerate for 1 hour.

When ready to cook the fish, drain the marinade and discard it.

To prepare the fish: In a heavy non-reactive skillet, heat the oil over medium heat. Add the shallots and sauté until wilted. Add the scallions, chives and garlic, and cook for 3 minutes. Add the tomatoes, chili pepper, parsley, bay leaf, thyme, and salt and pepper to taste; cook for 4 minutes. Add the fish and cook for 2 minutes. Pour in the coconut milk and bring to a simmer.

Arrange a fish fillet with some of the sauce in each of 4 shallow bowls. Serve with the halved limes.

Serves 4

Stewed Mako Shark

Islanders use names like "lion" and "old Jim" for their favorites among the several kinds of edible local shark. Stateside, mako is the lone shark entry on the bill of seafare.

4 mako shark steaks (about 6 ounces
   each) or swordfish or kingfish steaks
Salt and freshly ground white pepper
Juice of 3 limes
2 tablespoons chopped fresh parsley
2 tablespoons chopped fresh thyme
2 tablespoons chopped chives
3 tablespoons dark rum
3 tablespoons olive oil
3 medium onions, thinly sliced
4 garlic cloves, crushed
4 medium tomatoes, peeled and sliced
2 small fresh chili peppers, seeded,
   deveined and chopped
¼ cup Light Fish Stock (page 107) or dry
   white wine

Lightly sprinkle the fish steaks with salt and pepper. Arrange them in a single layer in a nonreactive dish. Sprinkle with half of the lime juice, all of the herbs and the rum. Refrigerate for at least 1 hour.

In a large nonreactive skillet, heat the oil. Add the onions and garlic, and sauté until lightly caramelized. Add the tomatoes and chili peppers, and cook for 10 minutes, or until the tomatoes give off most of their juice.

Add the fish steaks and stock to the skillet. Cook for 5 to 8 minutes, or until the steaks are just cooked through.

Serves 4

Orange Fish

This recipe was improvised by a Caribbean friend who had received a fresh snapper—just in time for lunch.

Olive oil
2 pounds snapper fillets, or other firm
   white fish, with skin intact
2 ripe avocados
Grated zest and juice of 1 orange,
   preferably Seville
2 tomatoes, sliced ¼ inch thick
Salt
Freshly grated nutmeg

Preheat the oven to 400° F.

Place a sheet of foil on a baking sheet and brush with olive oil. Place the fish fillets, skin-side down, on the foil. Peel the avocados and cut into thin slices. Arrange a thin layer of avocado slices over the fish. Sprinkle with the grated orange zest. Add a layer of tomato slices and pour the orange juice over the tomatoes. Season with salt to taste and dust with a few gratings of nutmeg.

Place another sheet of foil over the fish and fold several times to seal the edges. Bake for 15 minutes.

Divide the fish fillets into 6 portions. Allow the skin-side of the fish to stick to the bottom of the foil when you transfer each portion of fish to its warm dinner plate.

Serves 6

baked Snapper with Green Sauce

More often than not, Caribbean cooks score fresh fish and pack the cuts with a mixture of herbs and spices or a marinade before cooking.

1 tablespoon unsalted butter
½ cup chopped parsley
3 tablespoons chopped fresh coriander
1 teaspoon chopped fresh oregano
   or ¼ teaspoon dried
3 scallions (including some of the green),
   chopped
4 garlic cloves, minced
½ teaspoon ground cumin
½ cup fresh lime juice
Salt and freshly ground pepper
1 red snapper (about 5 pounds), cleaned
   and gutted, with head and tail intact
2 pounds cassava or potatoes, peeled
   and thinly sliced
½ cup olive oil
1 Scotch bonnet or fresh red chili pepper,
   seeded, deveined and minced
1 tablespoon minced parsley
Green Sauce (page 137)

Preheat the oven to 400° F. Butter an ovenproof dish large enough to hold the fish comfortably.

In a small bowl, combine the parsley, coriander, oregano, scallions, garlic, cumin, lime juice, and salt and pepper to taste. Score the fish 4 times on each side, cutting about ⅛ inch deep. Rub the mixture into the skin and cavity of the fish. Cover and refrigerate for 1 hour.

Arrange the cassava slices on the bottom of the baking dish and sprinkle half the oil and half the chili pepper on top. Place the fish on top. Drizzle the remaining oil and chili pepper over the fish. Cover with foil and bake for 40 to 45 minutes, or until the flesh is opaque and slightly flaky.

Transfer the fish to a serving platter, arrange the cassava around the fish and sprinkle with the minced parsley.

Serve with Green Sauce.

Serves 6

Skillet Snapper in Black Bean & Ginger Sauce

This dish reflects the Chinese contribution to island cooking. Fresh coriander —sometimes called Chinese parsley—is prevalent in many dishes, and before the cultivation of domestic ginger, resident cooks used a wild variety.

1½ tablespoons jarred or canned
    fermented black beans
2 teaspoons grated fresh ginger
2 large garlic cloves, crushed
1 teaspoon sugar
1 tablespoon dry sherry
3 tablespoons soy sauce
2 tablespoons Oriental sesame oil
½ cup Light Fish Stock (page 107)
¼ cup peanut oil
1 whole red snapper or other firm
    white fish such as black or striped
    bass (about 1½ pounds), gutted
    and scaled
Salt and freshly ground pepper
1 medium tomato, peeled, seeded and
    chopped
4 scallions (including some of the green),
    trimmed and finely sliced
1 tablespoon chopped fresh coriander

In a food processor, pulse the beans, ginger and garlic to a smooth paste. Add the sugar, sherry, soy sauce, sesame oil and fish stock. Puree until smooth.

In a large cast-iron skillet, heat the peanut oil. Season the fish with salt and pepper. When the oil is very hot, add the fish and quickly brown, about 15 seconds per side.

Pour the pureed bean sauce around the fish. Cover and simmer, basting 2 or 3 times, for 5 to 7 minutes or until the fish is opaque and flaky.

Transfer the fish to a warm platter. Pour the sauce over the fish and sprinkle with the chopped tomato, scallions and coriander. Serve immediately.

Serves 2 to 3

Buccaneer Fish

Seaside picnics are a favorite way to entertain in the islands. The food is usually prepared on the spot on a makeshift grill. More often than not, the main dish is the catch of the moment, marinated in a zesty sauce and served with tangy hot Sauce Ti-Malice.

2 pounds snapper, grouper or other firm
    white fish fillets, with skin intact
Salt and freshly ground pepper
⅓ cup olive oil
¼ cup fresh lime juice
2 thyme sprigs, or ½ teaspoon dried
⅛ teaspoon dry mustard
Sauce Ti-Malice (page 135)

Season the fish fillets with salt and pepper. Place in a large dish. Combine the oil, lime juice, thyme and dry mustard; pour over the fish. Cover and refrigerate for 1 hour, turning once.

Prepare a charcoal grill. When the coals burn with a dusty glow, lightly oil the grill. Arrange the fillets, skin side down, on the grill and cook for 2 to 3 minutes. Turn and cook for 2 or 3 minutes on the second side, or until just cooked through. Serve with Sauce Ti-Malice.

Serves 4

Fried Flying Fish

Sweet and tender flying fish are in our markets more and more. If you can't find it, lemon sole is a good substitute.

2 shallots, minced
1 tablespoon chopped chives
1 garlic clove, minced
¼ cup chopped red bell pepper
1 teaspoon chopped fresh thyme, or
    ½ teaspoon dried
⅛ teaspoon ground allspice
Salt
8 flying fish fillets, or substitute 1 pound
    lemon sole fillets
Juice of 2 limes
¼ cup vegetable oil
All-purpose flour, for dusting
2 eggs, lightly beaten

In a bowl, combine the shallots, chives, garlic, bell pepper, thyme, allspice, and salt to taste; set aside.

Score the fillets 2 or 3 times about ⅛ inch deep. Place the fillets in a non-reactive pan, pour on the lime juice, cover and refrigerate for 15 minutes.

Drain the fillets and pat dry with paper towels. Rub the seasoning mixture into the scored fish and set aside.

In a large cast-iron skillet, heat the oil over medium-high heat until it shimmers. Dust the fillets with flour and coat with the egg mixture. Dust with flour again. Fry the fish in the oil until golden, about 1 or 2 minutes on each side. Drain on paper towels.

Serve immediately, with Caribbean hot sauce.

Serves 2

Kingfish with Coo-coo

Kingfish should be well seasoned and poached, sautéed or steamed, since frying and grilling tend to dry it out.

6 kingfish steaks (5 to 6 ounces each)
2 tablespoons minced fresh parsley
2 tablespoons minced fresh thyme
2 tablespoons minced fresh oregano
1 teaspoon cayenne pepper
Salt and freshly ground pepper
Juice of 1 lime
3 tablespoons peanut oil
1 medium onion, finely chopped
2 garlic cloves, crushed
All-purpose flour, for dusting
½ cup Light Fish Stock (page 107)
1 cup dry white wine
2 teaspoons hot pepper sauce
1 tablespoon tomato paste
Cornmeal Coo-coo and Okra (page 114)

Season the fish steaks with the herbs, cayenne, salt and pepper. Arrange the steaks in a large nonreactive dish and sprinkle with the lime juice. Refrigerate for 1 hour.

In a large skillet, heat half of the oil over medium heat. Add the onion and garlic and sauté until wilted, about 10 minutes. Remove the onion mixture from the pan and reserve. Add the remaining oil to the pan and leave over medium heat.

Dust the fish steaks with flour. Place the fish in the hot skillet and brown for 2 minutes on each side.

Meanwhile, add the fish stock, wine, hot sauce and tomato paste to the onion mixture and blend. Pour the onion mixture over the fish steaks. Cover and simmer for about 8 minutes, or until the fish is just cooked through.

Serve with Cornmeal Coo-coo and Okra.

Serves 6

Shrimp Curry

This Trinidadian favorite combines East Indian influences and West Indian flavor. It is traditionally served with roti.

½ cup olive oil

1 pound medium shrimp, peeled and deveined

2 medium onions, chopped

3 garlic cloves, finely chopped

2 tablespoons grated fresh ginger

2 teaspoons curry powder

½ teaspoon ground turmeric

2 large ripe tomatoes, peeled, seeded and chopped

1 teaspoon tomato paste

2½ cups Light Fish Stock (page 107) or chicken stock

½ cup fresh Coconut Milk (page 139) or canned unsweetened

Salt

In a large nonreactive sauté pan, heat half the olive oil over medium heat. Add the shrimp and sauté for about 2 minutes, or until pink. Remove the shrimp with a slotted spoon and reserve.

Add the onions and a little more of the oil and cook until the onions are translucent. Add the garlic, ginger, curry powder and turmeric; mix thoroughly and cook for about 3 minutes.

Stir in the tomatoes, tomato paste, stock and coconut milk, and bring to a boil. Add salt to taste, reduce the heat and simmer for 30 minutes. Add the shrimp and cook for 2 minutes, or until just heated through.

Serve with boiled white rice or Roti (page 117).

Serves 4

Shrimp & Papaya Salad

Although the composed salad is rarely served in the islands, every once in a while a local cook will concoct a refreshing dish of cool vegetables or fruit with a fish or meat filler.

Salt
2 pounds medium shrimp
8 ounces bean sprouts
2 cups shredded Chinese cabbage
2 christophines (chayotes)
1 small papaya, peeled, seeded and
    cubed
2 tablespoons plum wine
2 tablespoons rice wine vinegar
½ cup vegetable oil
1 tablespoon Oriental sesame oil
½ cup chopped fresh mint
¼ cup chopped fresh coriander

In a pot of lightly salted boiling water, cook the shrimp for 3 minutes. Remove the shrimp and cool under cold running water. Shell and devein the shrimp; set aside.

In a pot of lightly salted boiling water, blanch the sprouts for 10 seconds. Remove and cool under cold running water. Drain thoroughly and set aside.

Blanch the cabbage in the same manner as the sprouts, cooking for 1 minute. Remove and drain thoroughly and set aside.

Peel the christophine. Blanch whole, cooking for 4 to 5 minutes, or until just crunchy. Drain and when cool enough to handle, cut in half. Remove the stringy pith in the center; cut the flesh into cubes and set aside.

In a large bowl, combine the shrimp, sprouts, cabbage, christophine and papaya. Cover and chill.

In a small bowl, whisk together the plum wine, rice wine vinegar, vegetable oil and sesame oil; season with salt to taste. Sprinkle the salad with the herbs and toss with the dressing.

Serves 4 to 5

Baked Tuna Caribe

Although this dish is usually served well done in the islands, I prefer the tuna to be pink. It is equally delicious at room temperature or incorporated into a fresh summer salad.

1 tuna steak (about 1½ pounds) or mako shark or swordfish, cut 1 inch thick
1 small red onion, sliced
2 rosemary sprigs, or 1 teaspoon dried
2 thyme sprigs, or 1 teaspoon dried
2 tablespoons chopped chives
3 garlic cloves, crushed
1 Scotch bonnet or small hot chili pepper, seeded, deveined and thinly sliced
1 cup dry white wine
About 2 cups olive oil
2 large tomatoes, peeled, seeded and chopped
Salt and freshly ground pepper
1 tablespoon drained capers

Preheat the oven to 225° F.

Place the tuna steak in an ovenproof dish that is just large enough to hold it tightly. Pack the onion, rosemary, thyme, chives, garlic and chili pepper into the dish. Pour in the wine and enough of the oil to almost cover.

Cover the baking dish with foil, set it in a baking pan and pour in boiling water to reach halfway up the sides of the dish. Bake for 45 minutes. Remove from the oven.

In a small nonreactive saucepan, heat the tomatoes and season with salt and pepper. Add the capers and warm through.

Slice the tuna into long, thin strips and spoon the sauce over the fish.

Serves 4

Crab Matoutou

Usually made with land crabs and served in the shells, this dish is served on a bed of lettuce with a dusting of cassava meal or bread crumbs.

2 tablespoons unsalted butter
½ cup cassava meal or bread crumbs
3 tablespoons olive oil
3 shallots, finely chopped
2 garlic cloves, minced
¼ teaspoon chopped fresh thyme
1 teaspoon minced Scotch bonnet pepper
    or fresh hot red chili pepper
Salt and freshly ground pepper
2 cups long-grain white rice
3½ cups Light Fish Stock (page 107)
3 tablespoons fresh lime juice
¼ cup fresh passion fruit juice, strained
1½ pounds lump crabmeat, picked clean
1 tablespoon chopped chives
1 tablespoon chopped parsley
1 head Bibb lettuce, washed and dried

In a small skillet, melt the butter over low heat. Add the cassava meal and toast until golden. Reserve.

In a nonreactive heavy casserole, heat the oil over medium heat. Add the shallots, garlic, thyme, chili pepper, and salt and pepper to taste. Sauté for 5 minutes.

Add the rice and stock. Cover and cook over low heat, stirring from time to time, until the rice is tender and all of the liquid is absorbed, 20 to 30 minutes. Stir in the fruit juices and cook for 5 minutes, or until the juices are absorbed. Toss in the crabmeat and cook until heated through. Mix in the herbs. Spoon the mixture over the lettuce leaves and dust with the reserved cassava.

Serves 6

Light Fish Stock

4 pounds assorted fish bones, including
    heads, tails and spines, from any
    white-fleshed fish such as snapper,
    grouper or bass
2 medium onions, chopped
3 celery ribs, roughly chopped
3 carrots, roughly chopped
2 teaspoons dried thyme
1 bay leaf
12 peppercorns
6 parsley sprigs
2 cups white wine
Cold water

Rinse the fish bones under cold running water, making sure the gills have been removed from the heads.

In a large stockpot, combine the bones, the remaining ingredients and enough cold water to cover.

Bring the stock to a boil and immediately reduce the heat to a simmer. Skim the stock and simmer gently for 20 to 30 minutes.

Line a strainer with a double thickness of dampened cheesecloth and place it over a large pot. Ladle the stock into the strainer and set aside until well drained, about 10 minutes. Do not press the juice from the solids.

Cool and refrigerate. The stock can be frozen in small containers.

Makes about 3 quarts

WEST INDIES

LONG

LONG before Columbus searched for his Eden and Cortez introduced the corn he discovered in Mexico to the rest of the world, the cassava, or yucca root, a rich brown tuber with barklike skin and starchy white flesh, was a staple of the people of the islands. This versatile plant—similar to and finer than couscous—forms the base for meal and flour as well as tapioca.

Corn probably came to the Caribbean in the sixteenth century. The native Indians ground the kernels into meal and began using it instead of cassava to make coo-coo—cousin to mush, polenta and spoon bread. In Barbados they add okra, a sure sign of African inspiration. Grenada, Puerto Rico and other islands serve coo-coo as well, but with the addition of coconut milk.

The classic team of rice and beans is popular on every island. This stick-to-your-ribs dish appears in many guises—Jamaicans cook it with coconut milk while others use it in a mélange with sweet peppers, tomatoes, bacon, smoked hock or salted beef. Rice and pigeon peas (*gandules*) make a favored combination in Trinidad and Jamaica. The famous *Moros y Cristianos* mixes big spoonfuls of black beans with snowy rice. Haiti serves up *riz au djon-djon*—rice cooked with local black mushrooms similar to dried Italian porcini.

Few Caribbean dishes are complete without rice and beans. *Sopa de gandules,* Puerto Rico's green pigeon pea soup, is flavored with *sofrito* and longaniza sausages, and Cuba's celebrated black bean soup, dark as chocolate, is always served with a side dish of fluffy rice and raw onions.

Like the corn of America, beans are part of the lore and strength of Caribbean cooking.

Moros y Cristianos

Black beans and white rice are a great favorite in Havana and Miami's Little Havana. Cubans often serve them for lunch and breakfast, invariably with fried eggs, fried ripe plantains and, of course, *salsa rojo*.

2¼ cups dried black beans, washed thoroughly but not soaked
4 cups fresh or canned chicken stock
Cold water
3 tablespoons olive oil
2 medium onions, finely chopped
2 garlic cloves, minced
1 medium green bell pepper, seeded and chopped
3 medium tomatoes, peeled, seeded and chopped; or 1½ cups canned plum tomatoes
1 bay leaf
Salt and freshly ground pepper
1½ cups long-grain white rice

Place the beans in a large stockpot and add the stock and enough cold water to cover by 2 inches. Bring to a boil, then reduce the heat and simmer for 1½ hours, or until just tender.

In a very large nonreactive sauté pan, heat the oil. Add the onions, garlic and bell pepper, and sauté until the onion is translucent. Add the tomatoes, bay leaf, and salt and pepper to taste. Drain the beans and reserve the liquid. Add the beans to the skillet. Cover and simmer for 10 minutes.

Stir in the rice and 1 cup of the reserved bean liquid. Bring to a boil and simmer over low heat, covered, until the moisture is absorbed and the rice is tender, about 20 minutes.

Serve with Salsa Rojo (page 136) or hot sauce.

Serves 6 to 8

Riz au Djon-djon
RICE WITH BLACK MUSHROOMS

This celebrated Haitian specialty is similar in taste and preparation to risotto.

1 ounce dried Haitian black mushrooms, or substitute European-type mushrooms such as porcini
2 cups hot water
4 tablespoons unsalted butter
1 small onion, minced
1 garlic clove, minced
2 cups long-grain white rice
About 3 cups fresh or canned chicken stock
1 teaspoon chopped fresh thyme, or ¼ teaspoon dried
Salt and freshly ground pepper

Place the dried mushrooms in a small bowl and cover with the hot water. Set aside for 30 minutes. Drain the mushrooms, strain the liquid and reserve. There should be about 1 cup.

In a heavy saucepan, melt the butter over medium heat. Add the onion and garlic, and sauté until the onion wilts. Add the rice and stir constantly, until the butter is absorbed.

Add the reserved mushroom liquid, stirring constantly. Add the stock, mushrooms, thyme, and salt and pepper to taste. Bring to a boil, cover and reduce the heat to very low. Cook for 20 to 30 minutes, or until the liquid is absorbed and the rice is fluffy and tender.

Serves 6

Dhal

These pureed cooked peas are a calming counterbalance to curry dishes, and they are a favorite roti stuffing.

2 cups split peas or lentils
4 cups water
1 teaspoon ground turmeric
Salt
2 tablespoons vegetable oil
1 medium onion, finely chopped
2 garlic cloves, chopped
1 teaspoon cumin seeds, crushed
Roti (page 117)

Soak the peas overnight, or until they are swollen. Drain.

Place the peas in a pot along with the water and turmeric. Cook for 15 minutes, or until tender. Season to taste with salt and set aside.

Heat the oil in a medium skillet over medium heat. Add the onion, garlic and cumin, and cook until the onion is tender and slightly browned. Fold the onion mixture into the peas. The mixture should be the consistency of hummus.

Serve with roti and curry dishes.

Makes about 2 cups

Cornmeal Coo-coo & Okra

Coo-coo is the grits of the Caribbean.

8 ounces fresh okra
1½ cups fresh or canned chicken stock
½ teaspoon salt
⅔ cup yellow cornmeal
3 tablespoons unsalted butter

Wash and trim the okra, and slice into ¼-inch thick rounds.

In a medium nonreactive saucepan, combine the stock, okra and salt, and bring to a boil. Reduce the heat and simmer for 8 minutes.

Pour in the cornmeal in a slow, thin stream, stirring constantly. Cook over medium heat, stirring, for about 5 minutes, or until the mixture is thick enough to pull away from the bottom and sides of the pan in a solid mass.

Spoon the mixture onto a heated and lightly buttered serving plate and shape it into a round cake about 1 inch thick. Spread the top with the butter. Serve immediately.

Serves 6

Congris
RED BEANS & RICE

Red beans are preferred by the Cubans from Santiago. Havanans, on the other hand, consider that all beans are black. Either kind is delicious, and this dish features the red.

2 tablespoons olive oil
1 medium onion, finely chopped
1 garlic clove, minced
2 medium tomatoes, peeled, seeded and chopped; or 1 cup canned plum tomatoes
1 bay leaf
Salt and freshly ground pepper
2 cups dried kidney beans, soaked overnight and drained
3½ cups fresh or canned chicken stock
1 cup long-grain white rice

In a nonreactive saucepan, heat the oil over medium heat. Add the onion and garlic, and sauté until the onion is translucent. Add the tomatoes, bay leaf and salt and pepper to taste. Bring to a simmer. Add the beans and stock, and bring to a boil. Reduce the heat and simmer for 1½ hours, or until the beans are almost tender, adding more stock or water if necessary and stirring from time to time.

Add the rice, cover and cook over low heat until the rice is tender and the liquid is absorbed, 20 to 30 minutes.

Serves 4 to 6

Fried Channa

Channa, or chick-peas, are served with curry dishes and are a popular snack food as well.

2 cups dried chick-peas, washed
½ cup vegetable oil
Salt
Cayenne pepper

Place the chick-peas in a large bowl. Add water to cover and set aside to soak overnight.

Drain the peas and remove the skins. Add cold water to cover and set aside to soak for 2 hours more. Drain and pat dry with paper towels.

In a cast-iron skillet, heat the oil until it shimmers. Add the chick-peas and fry until golden. Remove with a slotted spoon and drain on paper towels.

Dust liberally with salt and cayenne pepper.

Serve warm, or store airtight.

Serves 4 or more

Pigeon Peas & Rice

This is a Caribbean delicacy. At New Year's, pigeon peas are served for good luck, like our hoppin John.

About 8 ounces ham hocks, cut into chunks
1 medium onion, finely chopped
3 garlic cloves, finely chopped
About 3½ cups fresh or canned chicken stock
1 teaspoon dried thyme
2 tablespoons chopped fresh parsley
2½ cups dried pigeon peas (gandules), soaked overnight
2 cups long-grain white rice
½ cup fresh Coconut Milk (page 139) or canned unsweetened
Salt and freshly ground pepper

In a large casserole, brown the ham hock chunks on all sides over medium heat. When they have rendered most of their fat, add the onion and garlic, and sauté until the onion is translucent.

Add the stock and bring to a boil over high heat. Add the thyme and parsley. Drain the peas and stir into the boiling liquid. Bring the mixture back to a boil. Reduce the heat and simmer for 45 minutes, or until the peas are almost tender.

Stir in the rice and coconut milk, and season with salt and pepper to taste. Simmer for another 20 minutes, or until the liquid has been absorbed and the rice and pigeon peas are tender.

Serve immediately.

Serves 8 to 10

bakes

These fried roll-like breads accompany stews, soups and salads.

2 cups all-purpose flour
1 teaspoon salt
1½ teaspoons baking powder
3 tablespoons margarine or lard
1½ teaspoons sugar
About ½ cup ice water
Vegetable oil, for frying

Sift together the flour, salt and baking powder. Add the margarine and rub in until the mixture is the consistency of cornmeal. Add the sugar and combine well. Gradually add enough ice water to make a soft dough. Turn out and knead lightly on a floured surface. Gather into a ball, wrap in plastic and refrigerate for about 30 minutes.

Pinch off pieces of dough about the size of a lemon. Roll each piece into a flattened round about ¼ inch thick.

In a large heavy skillet, heat enough oil to cover the bakes by ½ inch. Fry a few at a time until golden brown on both sides.

Makes 10 to 12 bakes

ccra

This particular fritter came to the islands via West Africa and is served with spicy soups and stews.

2 cups dried black-eyed peas
2 Scotch bonnet peppers, seeded and diced
Salt
Vegetable oil, for frying

Place the peas in a large bowl, add water to cover and set aside to soak overnight.

Drain the peas and remove the skins. Add cold water to cover and set aside to soak for 2 hours more. Drain and pat dry with paper towels.

In a food processor, pulse the black-eyed peas until coarsely chopped. Add the chili pepper and salt to taste and continue to pulse until the mixture is fluffy.

In a heavy skillet, heat ½ inch of oil until it begins to shimmer. Drop the mixture by teaspoonfuls into the oil and fry on both sides until golden. Drain on paper towels and continue frying in batches until all of the batter is used. Serve warm.

Serves 6

Roti

Omnipresent street food, these floppy, flaky golden breads are folded like envelopes and filled thick with meat, fish or vegetable curries.

2 cups all-purpose flour
1 teaspoon salt
1 teaspoon baking powder
2 tablespoons unsalted butter, cut into
    bits
About ⅔ cup ice water
Vegetable oil, for frying

In the bowl of a electric mixer, sift together the flour, salt and baking powder. Add the butter and beat the mixture until it is the consistency of cornmeal. Gradually add the ice water until the dough forms a stiff, but not sticky, ball. Cover the dough with a clean kitchen towel and set aside for 45 minutes.

On a lightly floured surface, knead the dough for 5 minutes. Divide the dough into 12 equal balls. Place on a lightly oiled pan or dish and cover; let rest for 30 minutes.

On a lightly floured surface, roll out each ball as thin as possible without tearing, 10 to 12 inches in diameter.

Heat a cast-iron skillet or griddle over medium-high heat. Lightly brush some of the oil over 1 side of the roti, place the roti in the pan and cook for 1 minute. Brush the top side of the roti with oil, turn and cook for 1 minute on the second side.

Keep the cooked rotis warm in a clean kitchen towel while you continue to cook the remaining rotis.

Serve warm, with curried dishes or filled with curry or Dhal (page 113) and eaten like a sandwich.

Makes about 12 rotis

Caribbean markets

have all the frenzied ambience of a party when you arrive late. Legs and arms flap to the beat of vendors spieling their wares over the din of congested traffic, honking horns and the distant sound of sidewalk bands. The shopper enters a chaotic world of hawkers who sell everything from live chickens, turkeys and turtles to fruits, vegetables and chewing gum.

What always strikes me is the intensity of the gaily dressed throng who sashay from stall to stall pinching the avocados, tomatoes and eggplants before they buy, gathering up raffia-tied bunches of scallions and herbs, onions and garlic, and choosing from the rivers of red, green and yellow chili peppers. What makes another impression is the panoply of produce in shapes and shades strange to the foreign eye, with equally unfamiliar names—dasheen, callaloo, plantain, calabaza.

Dasheen and malanga are edible tubers that produce large heart-shaped leaves called *callaloo,* a taste-cousin to spinach. The leaves of these two distinct plants are used interchangeably, and are the main ingredient of—as well as giving the name to—what is surely the most famous of all island soups. As a vegetable, callaloo is boiled, then pureed—and cooked again with stock and coconut milk.

Plantain, or cooking banana, is a vegetable staple, similar in shape to the dessert banana, but dense, starchy and far less sweet. Plantains ripen at room temperature, just like the banana, but are cooked at various degrees of ripeness. Dark red or brown-ripe plantains are stuffed with spicy meats or shellfish and then fried and served with drinks; yellow or medium-ripe plantains are sautéed in butter and served as a side dish; and green plantains are boiled to accompany meat and fish, or fried and offered as an alternative to the potato chip.

Cassava and corn are a pair of starchy standards. Boiled, *cassava* has a pleasant though slightly bland flavor, something like a potato, and is a frequent accompaniment to meat dishes. Eaten alone, it's best with a little salt, ground pepper and lime juice. Corn on the cob is lathered with a paste of chili pepper and spices before grilling, cut raw into chunks and added to soups and stews, or grated and stewed with okra.

Other island standbys include the *calabaza,* or West Indian pumpkin, with firm, bright flesh; the pear-shaped *christophine,* or chayote, with crisp white flesh and zucchini-like taste; and the thick-skinned *Caribbean yam.* Pureed, boiled garlic laced with olive oil and seasoned with salt and pepper brightens the boiled yucca, yams and sweet and white potatoes that complement plain-cooked meats and fowl.

When it comes to method, one grand old Guadeloupean cook I know has a single strict rule: vegetables that grow below ground are cooked with the lid on, those that grow above, with the lid off. Considering the quality of what emerges from her kitchen, it's a rule I'd never contest.

Corn & Okra Stew

Known to the Islanders as "lady's fingers," okra came to the Caribbean with the early African arrivals.

2 cups fresh or canned chicken stock
Salt
12 large okras, about 1 cup, stems
    removed, cut into ¼-inch rounds
2 cups grated fresh sweet corn kernels
    and pulp (scraped off cobs)
2 tablespoons unsalted butter

In a saucepan, bring the stock to a boil. Add salt to taste and the okra. Cover and cook for 10 minutes.

Add the corn and cook, stirring, until the mixture is thick and creamy. Stir in the butter and serve hot.

Serves 6

Grilled Corn

Chili peppers and spice—used instead of butter, salt and pepper—give Caribbean character to corn on the cob.

6 ears fresh sweet corn
1 Scotch bonnet or jalapeño chili pepper,
    seeded
1 tablespoon whole black peppercorns
1 teaspoon thyme, or 2 teaspoons dried
2 teaspoons chopped fresh coriander
2 garlic cloves, peeled
2 tablespoons olive oil
½ teaspoon salt

Preheat a charcoal grill.

Meanwhile, pull down the corn husks but don't remove them. Remove the silk and rewrap the husks around the ears of corn. Soak the corn with the husks in cold water for 30 minutes.

In a food processor, combine the chili pepper, peppercorns, thyme, coriander, garlic, olive oil and salt, pulsing on and off until the mixture is a paste.

Remove the corn from the water, pull back the husks and drain thoroughly. Spread the paste over the kernels. Replace the husks.

Arrange the corn on the hot grill. Cook, turning often, for about 15 minutes, or until the husks are lightly charred. Serve in the husks.

Serves 6

Corn Pudding

Popular in the English-speaking islands, corn puddings are served with roasts and meat stews and as a first course.

2 tablespoons unsalted butter
3 eggs
1 tablespoon sugar
1 teaspoon salt
2 cups milk
2 cups fresh corn kernels and pulp
  (scraped off the cobs)
⅓ cup finely chopped onion
3 tablespoons unsalted butter, melted
⅛ teaspoon ground nutmeg

Adjust an oven rack to the middle shelf and preheat the oven to 350° F. Use the 2 tablespoons butter to generously coat a 1½-quart casserole; set aside.

In a large bowl, lightly whisk the eggs. Whisk in the sugar, salt and milk. Stir in the corn and onion. Add the melted butter and mix. Pour the mixture into the casserole and sprinkle with the nutmeg.

Place the casserole in a roasting pan and set in the oven. Add boiling water to reach halfway up the side of the casserole. Bake for 45 minutes, or until a sharp knife inserted into the center comes out clean. Serve immediately.

Serves 6 or more

Orange-Spiced Carrot Sticks

These sweet-and-pungent carrots are a favorite in the English-speaking islands.

¾ cup fresh orange juice
1 tablespoon light brown sugar
¼ teaspoon ground ginger
Freshly ground pepper
3 cups carrot julienne
Chopped fresh parsley and fresh
  coriander, for garnish

Combine the orange juice, brown sugar, ginger, pepper to taste and the carrot julienne in a medium nonreactive saucepan. Cover and cook over medium heat until the carrots are crisp-tender.

Sprinkle the parsley and coriander on top and serve hot.

Serves 6

Heart of Palm & Tomato Stew

The native Florida Sabal palm is now being farmed to supply the increasing demand for fresh heart of palm.

1 pound fresh heart of palm, or 1 can (14 ounces)
Salt
3 ounces salt pork, diced (about ⅓ cup)
1 medium onion, chopped
1 large ripe tomato, peeled, seeded and chopped; or 2 cups canned plum tomatoes
¼ teaspoon curry powder
Freshly ground pepper

Remove and discard the pink outer covering of the palm heart. Cut the fresh heart into 1-inch strips. Place the strips in a large bowl of salted water and set aside to soak for 20 minutes.

In a nonreactive saucepan, sauté the salt pork over medium heat until golden. And the onion and sauté until translucent. Add the tomato, curry powder, and salt and pepper to taste. Bring to a simmer.

Meanwhile, drain the palm strips and pat dry with paper towels. Add to the tomato mixture and simmer for about 12 minutes, or until the palm is tender.

Serves 4

Pumpkin Curry

Although calabaza is available at all West Indian markets, winter squash can be substituted.

3 tablespoons vegetable oil
1 medium onion, chopped
2 garlic cloves, chopped
2 tablespoons curry powder, or more to taste
Seeds from 2 cardamom pods
½ teaspoon ground allspice
1 red bell pepper, seeded and diced
1 bay leaf, crushed
2 medium tomatoes, peeled and chopped; or 1 cup canned plum tomatoes
1½ pounds calabaza (West Indian pumpkin) or winter squash, peeled, seeded and cut into 1-inch cubes
About 1 cup fresh or canned chicken stock
Salt and freshly ground pepper

In a large nonreactive heavy skillet, heat the oil over medium heat. Add the onion, garlic and curry powder, and cook, stirring, until the onion is wilted and translucent, about 5 minutes.

Add the cardamom, allspice, bell pepper and bay leaf, and cook for 2 more minutes. Add the tomatoes, calabaza, chicken stock, and salt and pepper to taste. Cover and cook over very low heat for 25 minutes, or until the calabaza is tender. Add a little more stock if the mixture begins to thicken.

Serve immediately.

Serves 6

Malanga Chips

Malanga, or yautia, is a shaggy vegetable sold at Puerto Rican and West Indian markets. These chips are as popular in the islands as in the States.

1 malanga (about 1 pound), or substitute sweet potatoes or white yams
Vegetable oil, for frying
Salt

Scrub the malanga and peel with a sharp paring knife. Set aside to soak in cold water for 10 minutes, as the vegetable tends to be slippery. Pat dry with paper towels.

Slice the malanga very thin with a sharp knife or on a mandolin. Place the slices in a bowl of cold water and reserve until you are ready to fry.

Heat the oil in a deep-fryer to 350° F. Drain the chips and *dry completely;* they cannot be wet. Test 1 chip for color and doneness. Fry in batches until golden. Drain on paper towels. Season the chips with salt and pepper.

Serves about 6

Stewed Cucumbers

Some Antillaise cooks add a pinch of curry to brighten this refreshing accompaniment to grilled fish and meats.

4 cucumbers, peeled, halved, seeded and cut into 1-inch slices
Salt
3 tablespoons olive oil
1 medium onion, finely chopped
2 large ripe tomatoes, peeled, seeded and chopped
1 medium yellow bell pepper, seeded and diced
⅛ teaspoon sugar
Freshly ground black pepper
½ teaspoon fresh lime juice
1 tablespoon snipped chives

Sprinkle the cucumber slices lightly with salt and set aside in a colander. Drain for 30 minutes or more.

In a medium nonreactive saucepan, heat the oil over medium heat. Add the onion and sauté until translucent. Press the water out of the cucumber slices and add to the onion. Add the tomatoes, bell pepper and sugar, and season with ground pepper. Cover and simmer for 30 minutes, or until the cucumbers are just translucent. Add the lime juice and sprinkle with the chives. Serve in small heated bowls.

Serves 6

Christophine with Tomatoes

Christophine (chayote) is a slightly bland vegetable that needs additional seasoning to enhance its very delicate flavor.

3 tablespoons olive oil
1 large onion, chopped
2 garlic cloves, minced
2 large christophine (chayotes), peeled
   and cut into ½-inch cubes
1 pound tomatoes, peeled and coarsely
   chopped
1 tablespoon chopped fresh basil
Salt and freshly ground pepper
2 tablespoons unsalted butter
⅓ cup dry bread crumbs
1 tablespoon chopped chives
½ cup grated Parmesan cheese

In a large skillet, heat the oil over medium heat. Add the onion and garlic and sauté until the onion is translucent, about 10 minutes.

Add the christophine, tomatoes and basil, and season with salt and pepper to taste. When the mixture begins to bubble, reduce the heat and simmer for 15 minutes, or until the christophine are tender. Stir from time to time. Pour the mixture into a baking dish and set aside.

In a small skillet, melt the butter over medium heat. Add the bread crumbs and sauté until golden brown. Reserve.

Preheat the broiler.

Sprinkle the chives, cheese and bread crumbs over the vegetable mixture. Place the baking dish under the broiler for 5 minutes, or until the surface is bubbling and golden. Serve immediately.

Serves 4

Gratin of Christophine

2½ pounds christophine (chayote), peeled
    and quartered
2 cups milk
2 egg yolks
1 tablespoon grated fresh ginger
1 tablespoon chopped chives
2 tablespoons heavy cream
2 tablespoons unsalted butter
Salt and freshly ground pepper
¼ cup grated Parmesan cheese
¼ cup dry bread crumbs

In a medium nonreactive saucepan, combine the christophine and milk, and place over high heat. Bring to a boil, reduce the heat and simmer until the christophine is tender, about 10 minutes. Drain.

Preheat the oven to 350° F. Generously butter a 2-quart baking dish.

In a food processor, purée the christophine and milk. Add the egg yolks and blend. Add the ginger, chives, cream, butter, and salt and pepper to taste; process until well mixed.

Turn the puree into the prepared baking dish. Sprinkle on the cheese and bread crumbs. Place on the upper oven rack and bake for 20 minutes, or until the surface is golden and bubbling.

Serves 6

Cassava Salad

This versatile Caribbean mainstay is a nice change from classic potato salad.

2 pounds cassava, peeled and cubed
½ cup mayonnaise
2 hard-cooked eggs, chopped
2 medium carrots, scraped, diced and
    cooked
1 small cucumber, peeled, seeded and
    diced
2 medium tomatoes, peeled, seeded and
    chopped
Salt and freshly ground pepper

Boil the cassava in lightly salted cold water to cover until fork-tender. Drain well and turn into a large bowl. Allow to cool.

Add the mayonnaise. Fold in the remaining ingredients and season with salt and pepper to taste.

Chill and serve.

Serves 6

Green Plantains au Gratin

Yellow to dark plantains have a more delicate and sweet taste and can also be used in this recipe, without the carrot.

½ lemon
1½ pounds green plantains
1 cup milk
1 cup grated cheddar cheese
1 small onion, grated
1 medium carrot, scraped and shredded
Salt and freshly ground pepper
3 eggs, separated
2 tablespoons unsalted butter
½ cup fresh bread crumbs
¼ cup freshly grated Parmesan cheese

Preheat the oven to 350° F. Generously butter a 1-quart soufflé dish.

Squeeze the lemon juice into a large pot of salted boiling water. Add the plantains in their skins and the lemon half and boil for 15 to 20 minutes, or until the plantain skins begin to burst. Drain and reserve.

In a nonstick saucepan, bring the milk to a boil over high heat. Whisk in the cheddar cheese, onion and carrot. Reduce the heat and stir until the cheese mixture is melted and creamy. Season with salt and pepper to taste; set aside.

In a food processor, puree the plantain pulp. Add the egg yolks and puree thoroughly. Reserve.

In a small skillet, melt the butter over medium heat. Add the bread crumbs and sauté until golden brown. Reserve.

With an electric mixer, beat the egg whites with a pinch of salt until stiff and glossy. Fold the plantain mixture into the cheese sauce. Gently fold in the egg whites.

Spoon the mixture into the prepared dish and dust with the bread crumbs and Parmesan cheese. Bake for 30 minutes, or until the top and sides are golden.

Serves 4

Banane Pésé
TWICE-FRIED PLANTAINS

This is a traditional accompaniment to Griots (page 71), the delicious pork bits served with Sauce Ti-Malice (page 135). *Tostones* is the Spanish-island name.

3 green plantains, peeled and cut
    diagonally into 1-inch pieces
2 tablespoons salt
Peanut or vegetable oil, for frying

In a large bowl, combine the plantains and salt, and add enough cold water to cover. Set aside for 1 hour. Drain the plantains and pat dry with paper towels.

In a large, heavy saucepan or deep-fryer, heat 3 inches of oil to 375° F. Fry the plantain slices about 8 at a time until golden brown. Drain on paper towels. Continue cooking in batches until all the slices are cooked.

Place the fried plantains between 2 sheets of wax paper and flatten with a mallet or rolling pin until about ⅛ inch thick.

Heat the oil again to 375° F. Refry the plantains, 4 at a time, turning once, until golden on both sides, about 1½ minutes per side. Remove with a slotted spoon and drain on paper towels. Serve hot.

Serves 6 to 8

Frituras de Name
FRIED YAM CAKES

Frituras can be made with many root vegetables, and give Caribbean ambience to any meal.

1 pound Caribbean yams (not sweet
    potatoes), peeled and finely grated
1 tablespoon unsalted butter, melted and
    cooled
2½ teaspoons finely grated onion
1 tablespoon minced fresh parsley
1¼ teaspoons salt
Freshly ground black pepper
2 egg yolks
3 tablespoons vegetable oil

Combine the yams, butter, onion, parsley, salt and a liberal grinding of pepper in a deep bowl, and mix well. Drop in the egg yolks and beat vigorously until somewhat smooth and thick enough to pull away from the sides of the bowl.

In a large, heavy skillet heat the oil over medium heat until almost smoking. Working in batches, drop about 1 tablespoon of the yam mixture into the hot oil. Cook for 4 to 5 minutes at a time, leaving enough space between the cakes for them to spread into 2- to 2½-inch rounds that are golden and crisp around the edges. Drain on paper towels. Keep the cooked cakes warm in a low oven while you fry the remaining batter. Serve hot.

Makes about 20 cakes; serves 6

Condiments
SAUCES
AND
SEASONINGS

Every

island presents a fiery array of bottled hot sauces and condiments. Some come charmingly packaged, with labels of Creole scenes and triangles of calico cotton gaily wrapped around their necks; others are put up simply in mason jars and sold at the local markets. Some are world-known, like Jamaican Pickapeppa Sauce or Bermudian Hot Pepper Sherry or Pepper Wine from Trinidad. They add flash to soups, stews, grilled meats and fish —and Hot Pepper Sherry gives a delicious punch to a Bloody Mary. Making these sauces and condiments is easy—and as much fun as cooking strawberry jam.

Hot sauces complement the endless variations of salt cod and vegetable fritters that often accompany preprandial cocktails in the islands. And rare is the dish that is eaten without some fiery sauce or other—even rarer is the locally celebrated cook who does not have his or her own whimsical alchemy to add to the steaming pot.

The seasonings used in most Caribbean dishes—largely the legacy of the French—include garlic, onions, thyme, chives and lime juice. They, and savory hot chili peppers, give Caribbean cooking its pungency and zing.

The chili pepper is part of a large, diverse family that ranges from the familiar sweet bell pepper to the jalapeño, habanero, finger and Scotch bonnet—which literally looks like a Scotsman's cap. Some of the oils in these demure looking peppers can be lethal. A sliver of chili pepper should be tasted before finding its way to the pot—just to get an idea of its thrilling, if deadening, effect. A warning to the cook whose tendency is to inhale the vapors from a batch of bubbling sauce: the aroma and steam may clear your sinuses but might blow your head off in the process!

Marinades delight the palate and add definitive flavor to pork, meat, chicken and fish. Both the ever-present *sauce chien* —a potpourri of spices, chili peppers and lime juice from the French islands—and the pungent *sofrito* from the Spanish islands enliven Caribbean cooking. And sweet-sour fruit relishes and chutneys can be the easy last-minute addition that puts a delectable island stamp on almost any dish.

Avocado Mayonnaise

Serve this rich and velvety sauce spread with cold shellfish or on cocktail toasts.

1 large avocado, peeled and pitted
1 fresh hot chili pepper, seeded
1 tablespoon parsley leaves
2 garlic cloves, crushed
3 scallions (including some of the green), trimmed and coarsely chopped
⅓ cup vegetable or olive oil
Juice of 1 large lime
Salt and freshly ground pepper

Combine the avocado, chili pepper, parsley, garlic and scallions in a food processor. Process to a puree. Gradually add the oil and beat well. Add the lime juice. Season with salt and pepper to taste.

Makes about 1½ cups

Mango Chutney

Spring and early summer—when mangos are ripe and cheap—is the time to make this truly special relish, which is a perfect accompaniment to curries, roasted meats and pork dishes.

3 cups distilled white vinegar
1½ cups packed dark brown sugar
3 cups chopped green mango
2 tablespoons coarsely chopped fresh ginger
6 medium onions, chopped
3 garlic cloves, chopped
1 fresh hot red chili pepper, seeded and chopped
2 tablespoons salt
½ cup fresh lime or lemon juice
1 cup raisins
½ cup currants

In a large nonreactive saucepan, bring the vinegar to a boil. Stir in the brown sugar and cook for 10 minutes or until dissolved. Add the mango, ginger, onions, garlic and chili pepper, and cook until the mango is soft.

Stir in the salt, lime juice, raisins and currants, and cook, stirring, until the mixture becomes the consistency of marmalade. Correct the seasoning.

Spoon the chutney at once into hot sterilized jars, leaving ¼-inch headspace. Wipe the jars' rims and seal immediately. Process in a boiling hot-water bath for 5 minutes after the water returns to a boil. Refrigerate after opening.

Makes 5 to 6 half-pints

Papaya & Banana Chutney

Chutneys add zest to Caribbean meals all year round.

1½ cups distilled white vinegar
2 cups packed dark brown sugar
1 large papaya, peeled, seeded and diced (about 2 cups)
2 large bananas, peeled and diced (about 2 cups)
2 tablespoons coarsely chopped fresh ginger
1 hot chili pepper, seeded and diced
1 cup sultana raisins
½ cup dark raisins
Salt

In a large nonreactive saucepan, bring the vinegar to a boil. Stir in the sugar and cook for 10 minutes, or until dissolved. Add the papaya, bananas, ginger and chili pepper, and cook over low heat until the fruit is soft, about 10 minutes.

Stir in the raisins and season with salt. Cook, stirring until the mixture becomes the consistency of marmalade.

Spoon the chutney into hot, sterilized, pint-size jars, leaving ¼-inch of head space. Wipe the jar rims and seal immediately. Process in a boiling-water bath for 5 minutes after the water returns to a boil. Refrigerate after opening.

Makes about 3 pints

Sauce Ti-Malice

Native to Haiti, this piquant foil for fried pork or chicken enhances grilled fish as well as plain meat dishes.

2 medium onions, finely chopped
2 shallots, finely chopped
½ medium red bell pepper, seeded, deveined and diced
1 medium tomato, peeled, seeded and chopped
⅔ cup fresh lime juice
3 tablespoons olive oil
About ⅛ teaspoon cayenne pepper
Salt and freshly ground white pepper

Combine all the ingredients in a glass jar. Cover and shake to blend. Refrigerate for 48 hours.

Serve at room temperature. Ti-Malice will keep in the refrigerator for up to 2 weeks.

Makes about 2 cups

Mango Relish

Green mangos are smaller and stringier than the smooth-textured larger variety —and make the most outstanding relishes and chutneys.

4 large green mangos
1 small onion, minced
2 tablespoons peanut oil
1 small fresh red chili pepper, seeded, deveined and diced
1 small green chili pepper, seeded, deveined and diced
Salt and freshly ground pepper

Peel the mangos. If stringy, use a 4-tined fork and scrape the flesh away from the pit, or grate the flesh against the wide holes of a grater.

Combine the mangos, onion, oil, chili peppers, and salt and pepper to taste in a jar. Cover and refrigerate for at least 2 hours. Serve the relish fresh. It will keep for 2 to 3 days in the refrigerator.

Makes about 2 cups

Salsa Rojo

This sweet-spicy condiment is a complement to black or red beans, black bean soup and any stew—and equally delicious on your favorite meatloaf.

½ cup olive oil
1 large ripe tomato, peeled, seeded and chopped
2 garlic cloves, chopped
4 scallions (including some of the green), chopped
1 medium red bell pepper, roasted, peeled and seeded; or 2 canned pimientos, drained
1 fresh hot chili pepper, seeded, deveined and chopped
1 teaspoon fresh oregano, or ¼ teaspoon dried
¼ teaspoon cayenne pepper
½ teaspoon sugar
½ cup tomato paste
Salt and freshly ground pepper
¼ cup white rum
1 tablespoon fresh lime juice

In a nonreactive saucepan, heat the oil over medium heat and add the tomato. Cook for 10 minutes. Add the garlic, scallions, bell pepper, chili pepper, oregano, cayenne, sugar, tomato paste, and salt and pepper to taste. Cook for another 15 minutes, or until the sauce is thick.

Add the rum and cook for 10 minutes. Remove from the heat and stir in the lime juice.

Allow to cool. Store in a tightly covered container and refrigerate. Keeps for 1 week or more.

Makes about 3½ cups

Green Sauce

Serve this with grilled prawns and lobster, as well as cold shellfish.

1 teaspoon dry mustard
3 garlic cloves
2 tablespoons capers, drained
2 hard-cooked egg yolks
2 tablespoons parsley leaves
2 tablespoons fresh coriander leaves
2 green tomatillos, husks removed and coarsely chopped
1/3 cup almonds or pine nuts, lightly toasted
Salt and freshly ground pepper
3/4 cup olive oil
Juice of 1 large lime or lemon

In a food processor, combine the dry mustard, garlic, capers, egg yolks, parsley, coriander, tomatillos, nuts, and salt and pepper to taste. Blend to a puree. Add the oil in a thin stream until emulsified and the sauce becomes the consistency of mayonnaise.

Add the juice and pulse until incorporated. Scrape the sauce into a container, seal and refrigerate.

Makes about 2½ cups

Sofrito

Sofrito is the tomato base of many meat dishes, stews and soups—and it can be added to most braised dishes.

8 ounces salt pork, cut in ¼-inch cubes
2 tablespoons annatto seed oil
4 medium onions, chopped
10 garlic cloves, chopped
2 medium green bell peppers, seeded, deveined and diced
2 pounds ripe tomatoes, peeled, seeded and chopped (about 2 cups)
2 oregano sprigs, or ½ teaspoon dried
1 tablespoon chopped fresh coriander
Salt and freshly ground pepper

In a large nonreactive skillet, sauté the salt pork over medium heat until golden. Remove the pork with a slotted spoon and drain on paper towels. Pour off most of the fat. Add the annatto oil, onions, garlic and bell peppers, and sauté over medium heat until the onions begin to sweat out their juices. Add the tomatoes, oregano, coriander and salt pork, and simmer over low heat for 30 minutes, stirring from time to time. Season with salt and pepper to taste.

Allow to cool. Store in a tightly covered container and refrigerate. It will keep for 1 week.

Makes about 2½ cups

Sauce Chien

On Martinique and Guadeloupe, Sauce Chien is as standard as a bottle of ketchup is in America. It can be used as a dip for salted cod fritters and boudin, as well as an accompaniment to grilled fish and meat dishes.

1 small onion, finely chopped
6 scallions (including some of the green), finely chopped
½ fresh chili pepper, cored, seeded and finely chopped
1 garlic clove, minced
Pinch of ground thyme
1 tablespoon finely chopped fresh parsley
Salt and freshly ground pepper
1 cup boiling water
Juice of 1 lime
2 tablespoons peanut oil

Combine the onion, scallions, chili pepper, garlic, thyme, parsley, and salt and pepper to taste in a large bowl. Add the boiling water and mix. Set aside until cool.

Stir in the lime juice and peanut oil. Taste and add more lime juice or oil as desired.

Store in a sealed container and refrigerate. Sauce Chien keeps for about 1 week.

Makes about 1½ cups

Colombo
CURRY POWDER

Many Caribbean cooks prepare their own curry powder. This one is typical of the French islands.

1 tablespoon whole cloves
1 tablespoon poppy seeds
2 tablespoons coriander seeds
1 tablespoon mustard seeds
¼ cup cumin seeds
1 dried hot pepper, pulverized
2 tablespoons ground cinnamon
5 tablespoons ground turmeric
2 tablespoons ground ginger
2 tablespoons garam masala

In a dry cast-iron skillet, toast the cloves, poppy seeds, coriander seeds, mustard seeds and cumin seeds over medium heat until the mustard seeds begin to pop. Allow to cool slightly.

Combine all the ingredients in a blender or mortar and grind into a powder. Store airtight.

Makes about 1¼ cups

Pepper Wine

Pepper vinegar can also be made following this method, substituting distilled vinegar for the rum or sherry.

6 fresh Scotch bonnet or hot red chili peppers, washed and dried with stem intact
2 cups light rum or dry sherry

Place the peppers in a 1-quart glass container and pour in the rum. Cover loosely with the lid and allow to stand for 10 days in a dark cool place before using. Screw the lid on tight and store.

Makes about 2 cups

Note: The chili peppers give off their heat in about 10 days and will not get hotter. If you find it too strong, test it on the fifth day; if you like the degree of hotness then, remove the peppers.

Coconut Milk

Freshly grated coconut and coconut milk are far superior to canned or packaged varieties.

1 coconut
2 cups very hot (almost boiling) water

Preheat the oven to 375° F.

Using a long, clean nail, tap through the two eyes of the coconut. Drain the liquid and reserve it for another use.

Set the coconut in a baking pan and bake for 10 minutes. Hammer around the equator of the coconut until it splits in half. Pry the meat loose from the shell; peel off the brown outer coating.

Cut the coconut meat into chunks. Combine in a food processor with 1 cup of the hot water and puree. Strain the liquid into a bowl; return the solids to the processor. Add the remaining 1 cup hot water and process for 1 to 2 minutes. Strain again, pressing down on the solids to remove the moisture. Discard the solids. Use the coconut milk within a day or two, or freeze.

Makes 2 to 2½ cups

guava

paste and cream cheese spread on crisp crackers serve the host well who wants to end his or her Caribbean meal on an authentic, if easy, note. But the true glory of island desserts is something that approaches the Garden of Eden: a cornucopia of fruits, from the familiar to the exotic. This kaleidoscopic array—colored the red of sunset, the deepest green of the rain forest and the blue of midnight—comes to the table in ice-filled bowls at the peak of ripeness, the perfect and pleasurable coda to a meal.

Fruits pervade the West Indian dessert list, flavoring ices, ice creams, puddings, mousses, pastries, sauces, candies, jams, jellies, cocktails and liqueurs—often with the accents of vanilla, cinnamon, clove, ginger or star anise. Their tastes can be delicate or strong, intensely sweet or with sweet-sour bite, pungent or subtle—intriguing and irresistible.

Papaya, mango, coconut, pineapple and passion fruit are now among the familiars in markets throughout the United States—and sometimes a rainbow of rarer island fruits are to be found, too. The carambola, or star fruit, mildly sour and slightly sweet, adapts well to desserts and salads. The pale green cherimoya's custardlike texture and creamy vanilla flavor is delicious on its own. Both, along with the densely sweet guava and the translucent lychee, are among the tropical exotics being grown in Florida and California today. Fresh fruits are available from greengrocers, purees and juices come frozen and bottled, and the Hispanic and Oriental markets often carry frozen pulp. In a pinch, the local Papaya King (a fast-food chain that specializes in hot dogs and tropical juices) supplies me here in New York with the coconut milk, papaya and mango juices that I freeze in my ice cream machine or serve with rum at the end of a hot summer's evening in the city.

When shopping locally for island fruits and vegetables, I take the advice of a Florida friend who always finds and follows a Cuban-born shopper in the markets of Miami. "Whatever she casts aside, I pick up and buy. It's the second-best choice. Eventually, I learn what she knows."

Chocolate Brittle Ice Cream

Though Islanders have a special fondness for ices and sherbets, they do some wonderful fruit and spice ice creams.

ICE CREAM
5 ounces bittersweet chocolate, cut into bits
2 tablespoons unsalted butter
¼ cup cold brewed espresso coffee
2 cups heavy cream
2 cups milk
1 star anise
½ vanilla bean
⅔ cup sugar
5 egg yolks

PRALINE
1 cup sugar
½ cup water
1 cup slivered almonds
¼ cup dark rum

To make the ice cream: In a medium saucepan, melt the chocolate with the butter over low heat. Stir in the espresso and set aside.

In a large saucepan, combine the cream, milk, star anise, vanilla bean and sugar. Cook, stirring, until the mixture lets off steam. Remove from the heat.

In a large bowl, whisk the egg yolks until well beaten. Slowly pour in the hot milk mixture. Return the mixture to the saucepan and whisk constantly over low heat until the custard begins to thicken, about 10 minutes.

Pour a little of the custard into the melted chocolate to warm it. Whisk the chocolate into the custard until very well blended. Set the pan in a bowl of ice and stir until cool. When cool, refrigerate until chilled.

To make the praline: In a small saucepan, combine the sugar with the water. Bring to a boil, stirring with a wooden spoon, until the sugar dissolves. When the sugar begins to caramelize and turn amber, fold in the slivered almonds. Pour the mixture onto a lightly oiled baking sheet and allow to cool. When cool, break the praline into small bits.

When the chocolate custard base is thoroughly chilled, remove the star anise and vanilla pod. Add the praline to the chocolate mixture and stir in the rum. Freeze in an ice cream maker according to the manufacturer's directions.

Makes about 1½ quarts

Honey-Braised Pineapple (with Mint Ice Cream)

Spiced fruit is a delicious counterpoint in taste and texture to mint ice cream.

1 large ripe pineapple
2 tablespoons ground cinnamon
1 tablespoon ground ginger
1 teaspoon ground mace
⅛ teaspoon ground cloves
⅛ teaspoon ground cardamom
½ cup sugar
8 tablespoons (1 stick) unsalted butter
⅔ cup dark honey

Preheat the oven to 375° F.

Peel the pineapple, cut lengthwise into quarters and cut away the core. Mix all the spices with the sugar and dust the pineapple with the mixture.

In an ovenproof skillet, melt the butter over medium heat. Add the honey and stir until melted and combined. Lightly brown the pineapple quarters on all sides in the butter-honey mixture. Place the pan in the oven and bake for about 20 minutes, or until the butter-honey mixture darkens and caramelizes.

Remove the pan from the oven and cut the pineapple into thin slices. Fan out the slices on the side of the dessert plates.

Spoon a little of the syrup over the fruit and place 1 or 2 small scoops of Mint Ice Cream (recipe follows) onto each plate.

Serves 6 to 8

Mint Ice Cream

3 cups milk
¾ cup sugar
1 piece (1 inch long) vanilla bean, split; or
  1 teaspoon vanilla extract
3 egg yolks
1 bunch fresh mint leaves, washed, dried and chopped (about 1 cup)
1 cup heavy cream

In a heavy saucepan, combine the milk, sugar and vanilla bean over medium-low heat. (If using vanilla extract, do not add it at this stage; wait until after chilling the mixture.) Stir with a wooden spoon until the sugar dissolves. Set aside.

In a large bowl, beat the egg yolks until they coat the whisk. Slowly whisk in the sweetened milk mixture. Add the chopped mint and continue to whisk until the mixture cools. Refrigerate until cold.

Strain the mixture through a fine sieve, pressing down on the vanilla bean and mint leaves to extract all of the moisture; discard the bean mint. Add the heavy cream to the custard.

Freeze in an ice cream maker according to the manufacturer's directions.

Makes about 1 quart

Coconut Ice

Fruit ices of every tropical flavor are sold day and night from gaily painted pushcarts. The vendor scrapes flakes of ice from a large block into a paper cup and pours sweet fruit syrup on top.

¾ cup sugar
4 cups fresh Coconut Milk (page 139)
1 cup heavy cream
¼ teaspoon vanilla extract

In a medium saucepan, melt the sugar in the coconut milk over medium heat, stirring constantly until the sugar dissolves. Stir in the cream and vanilla. Pour into a container and refrigerate until cold

Freeze the mixture in an ice cream maker according to the manufacturer's directions.

Makes 1 quart

Lime Sherbet

½ cup fresh lime juice
1½ cups sugar syrup (see Pineapple Sorbet, opposite)
1 tablespoon lightly beaten egg white
¼ cup triple-lime liqueur (optional)

In a bowl, combine the lime juice, sugar syrup and egg white. Chill well.

Freeze until almost set in an ice cream maker, according to the manufacturer's directions.

About 10 minutes before the sherbet is frozen, add the liqueur and continue processing. Allow to ripen for 1 hour in the freezer before serving.

Makes 1 pint

Pineapple Sorbet

1 large pineapple, trimmed, cored and cut
   into chunks
About 2 cups sugar (depending on the
   sweetness of the fruit)
2 cups water
2 tablespoons vodka or rum

In a food processor, blend the pineapple chunks until smooth. Strain; discard the pulp and reserve the juice.

In a nonreactive saucepan, combine the sugar and water. Bring to a boil over high heat, stirring with a wooden spoon, until the sugar dissolves. Continue boiling for 5 minutes, then remove from the heat and set the sugar syrup aside to cool.

Add enough of the sugar syrup to the pineapple juice to sweeten it. Stir in the vodka. Refrigerate until cold.

Freeze in an ice cream maker according to the manufacturer's directions.

Makes about 1 quart

Soursop Ice Cream

2¼ cups heavy cream
2 cups sugar
1½ cups seeded soursop pulp

In a medium saucepan, heat the cream and sugar until the sugar dissolves and the mixture lets off steam. Remove from the heat. Pour into a bowl and set aside to cool.

When cool, mix in the soursop pulp. Refrigerate until chilled.

Freeze in an ice cream maker according to the manufacturer's directions.

Makes about 1 quart

Bananarama

This mix of yogurt, cream and bananas is adapted from a recipe that was given to me by James Beard.

5 large ripe bananas
Juice of 1 lemon
1 cup superfine sugar
2 cups plain yogurt
1 cup heavy cream, whipped to soft peaks
2 tablespoons dark rum

In a food processor, puree the bananas with the lemon juice. Add the sugar and pulse on and off until incorporated. Scrape the mixture into a large bowl. Fold in the yogurt. Gently fold in the whipped cream and rum; do not over-mix.

Scrape the mixture into an ice cream maker and freeze according to the manufacturer's directions.

Makes about 1 quart

Tooloom

From Puerto Rico to Barbados to Martinique, there are myriad varieties of coconut candies. These are especially good served with fruit ices.

1 cup packed dark brown sugar
¼ cup molasses
2½ cups grated fresh coconut
1 tablespoon grated orange zest
1½ teaspoons grated fresh ginger

Place the brown sugar in a heavy non-reactive saucepan over medium heat and stir until it liquefies. Add the molasses and stir briskly. Fold in the coconut, orange zest and ginger. Reduce the heat and stir until the mixture pulls away from the sides of the pan, about 12 minutes. Remove from the heat and set aside to cool.

Lightly oil a baking sheet. Using a teaspoon, drop the mixture onto the sheet one spoonful at a time. Cover with plastic wrap until ready to serve.

Toolooms may be individually wrapped and stored in plastic wrap for up to 1 week.

Makes about 2 dozen

Coconut Confiture

The celebrated Creole cook Madame Violetta serves this spectacular syrup over vanilla ice cream in her popular Guadeloupe restaurant.

1 cup sugar
1 cup water
½ cup dark rum
⅛ teaspoon ground cinnamon
A few gratings of nutmeg
1 vanilla bean, split
1½ cups freshly grated coconut meat

Combine the sugar with the water in a nonreactive saucepan and bring to a boil over high heat. Stir with a wooden spoon until the sugar dissolves. Reduce the heat to low and add the rum, cinnamon, nutmeg and vanilla bean. Simmer until the liquid reduces to a heavy syrup, 15 to 20 minutes.

Stir in the grated coconut and cook for 5 minutes, or until the coconut is tender.

Discard the vanilla bean; set the mixture aside to cool. Serve over vanilla ice cream. To store, refrigerate in a sealed container.

Makes about 1 quart

Mango Fool

Fruit fools are an enduring British legacy to the Caribbean. Any thick tropical fruit puree can be substituted for the mangos in this recipe.

4 to 5 mangos, peeled and pitted
2 tablespoons fresh lime juice
3 tablespoons dark rum
⅛ teaspoon ground cinnamon
2 dashes Angostura bitters
About ½ cup superfine sugar
1 cup heavy cream, whipped to stiff peaks
  and chilled

In a food processor, puree the mango pulp with the lime juice, rum, cinnamon, bitters, and sugar to taste. Do not overblend. Cover and chill thoroughly.

Just before serving, gently fold in the whipped cream.

Serves 6

Bread Pudding

This British import has long been part of the Caribbean dessert repertoire. Ingredients may change slightly, and every island has a variation.

PUDDING
6 tablespoons unsalted butter
12 ounces white Italian bread, cubed
4 cups milk
1 cup heavy cream
½ vanilla bean, split
1 cinnamon stick
8 egg yolks
⅛ teaspoon salt
1 cup sugar

SYRUP
1 cup sugar
¼ cup water
½ cup dark rum

To make the pudding: Melt the butter in a large skillet over medium heat. Add the bread cubes and toast until golden. Remove from the heat and set aside.

In a heavy saucepan, bring the milk, cream, vanilla bean and cinnamon stick to a boil.

Meanwhile, in a bowl, beat the egg yolks with the salt and sugar. Add the boiling milk mixture and stir constantly until well combined. Remove the cinnamon stick and vanilla bean.

Place the cubed bread in a large bowl. Pour the milk mixture over the bread cubes; set aside for 30 minutes.

To make the syrup: In a small saucepan, combine the sugar with the water. Cook until the sugar dissolves and the syrup turns golden. Stir in the rum.

Pour the syrup into a 12-inch square baking pan or casserole. Swirl the pan to coat with syrup. Cool.

Preheat the oven to 325° F.

Pour the soaked bread mixture over the syrup. Place the pan in a roasting pan on the middle shelf of the oven. Pour in boiling water to reach halfway up the side of the pan. Bake for 1 hour, or until lightly browned and set.

Serves about 6

Sponge Cake

In the Caribbean, sponge cake usually appears at the tea table, or decorated in riotous colors for birthdays. I like it best after a meal—à la mode.

CRUST
3 tablespoons granulated sugar
3 tablespoons all-purpose flour

CAKE
6 eggs, separated
½ cup cold water
1½ cups granulated sugar
½ teaspoon vanilla extract
½ teaspoon orange or lemon extract
1½ cups all-purpose flour
¼ teaspoon salt
¾ teaspoon cream of tartar
⅓ cup guava or passion fruit preserve
Confectioners' sugar

Preheat the oven to 350° F. Grease two 10-inch round cake pans.

To make the crust: Combine the sugar and flour. Dust the greased pans with the mixture until coated evenly. Reserve the remaining crust mixture.

To make the cake: In the bowl of an electric mixer, beat the egg yolks until thick and lemon colored. Add the cold water and continue beating until thick. Gradually beat in the granulated sugar. Beat in the vanilla and orange extracts.

Sift the flour with the salt 3 times. Fold into the egg yolk mixture a little at a time.

Beat the egg whites with the cream of tartar until stiff peaks form. Fold into the batter.

Divide the batter between the cake pans. Sprinkle the reserved crust mixture on top.

Bake for about 1 hour, or until golden. Invert the pans on a rack for 10 minutes. Then remove the pans and let the cakes cool completely on the rack.

Spread the preserves on top of one layer and set the other layer on top. Dust the top with confectioners' sugar.

Serves 10

Boniatillo

All the children of the Spanish-speaking islands are crazy about this deliciously sweet-spiced pudding.

1 pound sweet potatoes, quartered
Salt
1½ cups sugar
Zest of 1 lime, cut in strips
½ cup cold water
3 eggs, separated
¼ cup medium-sweet sherry or amber rum
¼ teaspoon ground mace
⅛ teaspoon ground ginger
2 to 3 dashes Angostura bitters

In a large saucepan, place the sweet potatoes in lightly salted water to cover, and bring to a boil over high heat. Cook for 30 minutes, or until fork-tender. Drain and peel the sweet potatoes.

In a heavy saucepan, combine the sugar and lime zest with the water. Bring to a boil over medium heat and continue to boil until the sugar dissolves. Remove the syrup from the heat and discard the zest.

In a large bowl, mash the sweet potatoes until smooth and mix in the syrup with a wooden spoon. Mix in the egg yolks, sherry, spices and bitters. Place the bowl over a saucepan of boiling water that will comfortably hold the bowl. Continue to stir until the mixture begins to thicken, about 10 minutes. Remove from the heat and set aside to cool.

With an electric mixer, beat the egg whites with a pinch of salt until stiff and glossy.

When the sweet potato puree is cool, add one-third of the egg whites and blend. Lightly fold in the remaining egg whites. Do not overblend. Refrigerate and chill slightly.

Serve cool with vanilla sauce or heavy cream.

Serves 4 to 6

Coco Quemado
COCONUT FLAN

Ending a meal with a custard or flan is a longtime tradition on all the Spanish-speaking islands. Don't be concerned if the custard separates after baking; the combination of coconut and custard does that.

1½ cups sugar
½ cup cold water
5 eggs, separated
2 cups milk
Grated zest of 1 navel orange
1 tablespoon amber or dark rum
2 cups grated fresh or packaged
    unsweetened coconut
Salt

Adjust the oven rack to the middle shelf and preheat the oven to 325° F.

In a heavy saucepan, bring 1 cup of the sugar and the water to a boil over high heat. Stir with a wooden spoon until the sugar dissolves. When the sugar begins to caramelize and the color is amber, pour the caramel into a 10-inch glass pie pan and rotate until the surface is evenly coated.

In a medium bowl, whisk the egg yolks until thick and lemon colored. In a saucepan, scald the milk and the remaining ½ cup sugar, stirring until the sugar dissolves. Gradually pour the milk mixture into the yolks, whisking constantly. Add the orange zest, rum and coconut. Cover and chill.

With an electric mixer, beat the egg whites with a pinch of salt until stiff but not dry. Gradually fold the egg whites into the cooled coconut mixture, then transfer to the caramel-coated pie pan.

Place the pie pan in a roasting pan and set on the oven rack. Pour boiling water into the roasting pan to reach halfway up the side of the pie pan. Bake for 1 hour, or until a paring knife inserted in the center comes out clean.

Serve the custard at room temperature with fresh fruit.

Serves 6

banana Beignets

The crisp-fried batter and creamy filling make these pastries favorites of all the French islands.

FILLING
4 ripe bananas
½ cup dark rum
3 tablespoons sugar
¼ teaspoon ground allspice
1 teaspoon vanilla extract

BATTER
2 eggs, separated
1 cup all-purpose flour
¼ teaspoon salt
½ teaspoon baking powder
1 tablespoon unsalted butter, melted
2 tablespoons dark rum
½ cup milk
Vegetable oil, for frying
Confectioners' sugar

To make the filling: Peel the bananas and cut each of them in half lengthwise.

Then cut each half into 4 equal pieces.

In a mixing bowl, lightly toss the banana pieces with the rum, sugar, ground allspice and vanilla. Cover the mixture and reserve.

To make the batter: In another mixing bowl, whisk the egg yolks. Sift in the flour, salt and baking powder. Add the butter, rum and milk.

In a medium bowl, whisk the egg whites with a pinch of salt until stiff and glossy. Fold into the batter.

In a deep-fryer or deep saucepan, heat the oil to 375° F. Coat the banana pieces with the batter a few at a time and fry until golden. Remove the banana pieces with a slotted spoon and drain on paper towels. Continue cooking beignets in batches until all of the banana pieces are used. Dust the beignets with confectioners' sugar.

Serve warm.

Serves 4 to 6

Mango Bread

Fruit breads are served as lunch or dinner desserts and are equally popular at island teatime.

2 cups all-purpose flour
2 teaspoons baking soda
2 teaspoons ground cinnamon
½ teaspoon salt
1 cup vegetable oil
1 cup granulated or brown sugar
3 eggs, lightly beaten
1 teaspoon vanilla extract
2 cups cubed ripe mango
¼ cup golden raisins (optional)
3 tablespoons shredded coconut
   (optional)

Grease and flour a 1-pound loaf pan.

Sift together the flour, baking soda, cinnamon and salt.

In a large mixing bowl, beat together the vegetable oil and sugar, blending well. Gradually stir in the flour mixture alternately with the eggs. Beat in the vanilla extract. Stir in the mango. Fold in the raisins and coconut.

Pour the batter into the prepared loaf pan and set aside to rest for about 20 minutes, or until the batter bubbles slightly. While the batter rests, preheat the oven to 350° F.

Bake the bread for 45 to 60 minutes, or until the top springs back when lightly pressed. Remove the bread from the pan; cool on a rack. Slice and serve as a snack or with vanilla ice cream or fruit sherbet.

Makes 1 loaf

Guava Buñuelos

These Cuban fruit crullers are favorites from Havana to Miami.

2½ cups all-purpose flour
¼ cup sugar
2½ teaspoons baking powder
1 teaspoon ground cinnamon
¼ teaspoon salt
1 egg
1½ cups milk
2 tablespoons unsalted butter, melted
1 can (16 ounces) guava halves, drained
   and chopped, with liquid reserved
Vegetable oil, for deep-frying
Cream cheese, for serving

In a bowl, sift together the flour, sugar, baking powder, cinnamon and salt. In another bowl, mix the egg, milk and butter. Add the liquids to the dry ingredients and whisk until completely incorporated. Add the chopped guava (but not the juice) and mix well.

In a deep-fryer, heat the oil to 375° F. Drop the batter by tablespoonfuls into the oil and fry until browned on all sides. Drain on paper towels. Continue frying in small batches until all of the batter is used.

Serve with cream cheese and the juice from the guavas.

Makes 32 buñuelos

Frozen Key Lime Mousse

The last thing I do on an island visit is buy a couple of bottles of lime juice—freshly squeezed, tart and pungent. It keeps for only a week or two, but that's long enough to remind me of the pleasures just past.

1½ teaspoons unflavored gelatin
½ cup key lime juice or lime juice
3 eggs, separated
⅔ cup sugar
Grated zest of 1 lime
Salt
1 cup heavy cream

In a nonreactive double boiler, stir the gelatin into the lime juice over medium heat. When the gelatin dissolves, set the mixture aside to cool.

In a large bowl, beat the egg yolks with ⅓ cup of the sugar until the mixture is smooth and lemon colored. Fold in the lime-gelatin mixture and the lime zest. Set aside.

In the bowl of an electric mixer, beat the egg whites with a pinch of salt. Gradually add the remaining ⅓ cup sugar and beat until the whites form stiff, glossy peaks.

Gently but thoroughly blend a large spoonful of the beaten whites into the lime-egg mixture. Whip the heavy cream to fairly firm peaks. Fold the remaining egg whites and the whipped cream into the lime-egg mixture. Do not overblend.

Freeze the mixture in an ice cream maker according to the manufacturer's directions.

Makes about 1½ quarts

ACKNOWLEDGMENTS

First thanks are due Helen McEachrane, my friend and colleague, who brought a delicious legacy and a priceless history of Caribbean cooking to this collaboration. And to Howard Gilman, Helen's mentor and friend—a big thank-you from both of us.

Also, to Cheryl Merser for being there once more—and to Eugenie Voorhees for constant encouragement and time off in the sun.

I especially want to thank Graciella Espino, Joe Petrocik and Myron Clement for their help and know-how when it comes to Cuba and the French West Indies. And thanks to Lauretta—the wonderful and luscious Martiniquaise—who knows that a Scotch bonnet pepper is vital but too hot to be used without discretion; and also to Catherine Chicate-Moibert, Guadeloupiane and tour guide nonpareil.

Once again, gratitude and thanks to recipe editor Mardee Haidin Regan and to computer whiz Steven Meisels, who rescues information magically.

And to Geraldine Stutz, a steadfast friend, our appreciation and thanks for all the time and the backstopping that helped make this book happen.

To Paula Munck, whose illustrations are the stuff dreams are made of, and to Elizabeth Van Itallie for designing this book—we thank you.

And to Howard Klein, Jane Treuhaft, Ed Otto, Mark McCauslin and the rest of the staff at Clarkson Potter, our thanks and appreciation.

index